*Missional Reset*

# Missional Reset

*Capturing the Heart for Local Missions in the Established Church*

DESMOND BARRETT
and CHARLOTTE P. HOLTER

Foreword by *Rodney Reed*

RESOURCE *Publications* · Eugene, Oregon

MISSIONAL RESET
Capturing the Heart for Local Missions in the Established Church

Resource Publications
An Imprint of Wipf and Stock Publishers
199 W. 8th Ave., Suite 3
Eugene, OR 97401

www.wipfandstock.com

PAPERBACK ISBN: 978-1-6667-7071-1
HARDCOVER ISBN: 978-1-6667-7072-8
EBOOK ISBN: 978-1-6667-7073-5

VERSION NUMBER 050123

I am thankful for the godly example of Judy Binkley, a former local missions president for the Lehigh Acres Church of the Nazarene, who taught me to strive for excellence in presenting missions to the church. She shared missions with passion, purpose, consistency, and creativity to capture the imaginations of the people. She did so to give towards a higher calling in sowing into God's plans for his kingdom.

—D.B.

I'm thankful for the responsiveness of my parents, Dr. and Mrs. Samuel Pickenpaugh, who answered a call to serve as specialized assignment missionaries to Australia for the Church of the Nazarene. Seeing the work of missions in action through their lived experiences solidified the importance of it. This shaped my life to always be active in missions whether it be in serving on the field or leading others to seek and do the missional call of God.

—C.P.H.

# Contents

# Foreword

MANY YEARS AGO, I read William Booth's book *In Darkest England and the Way Out*. Published in 1890, it was Booth's critique of the failure of the churches of England to reach the new urban masses who lived in utter poverty and what he perceived as the remedy for it. This work by Dr. Barrett and Dr. Holter reminds me of Booth's work. Barrett and Holter have given the church a manifesto on the issue of the church's mission. They argue persuasively that the church in North America is generally failing in its mission of sharing the love of Christ to those in need in its local context. They have correctly identified that while most churches have tried to continue with ministry practices that may have worked thirty or forty years ago, the world has moved on.

Churches that were established by founders who had a robust vision for local missions, have now become social clubs, designed to meet the needs of only the aging "members" and not communities that currently exist around them. While not undermining the need to continue to invest in global missions, this book is mostly about investing in local missionary activity. Barrett and Holter not only diagnose the problem but go on to offer insightful solutions to the problem based on their research, experiences, and observations. As one whose career has been given to cross-cultural ministry, I strongly recommend this book to anyone who desires for their church to be truly mission-driven both locally and internationally.

Dr. Rodney Reed
Global Missionary of the Church of the Nazarene serving as Deputy Vice Chancellor of Academic and Student Affairs, Africa Nazarene University, Nairobi, Kenya

# Introduction

WHAT MAKES YOUR CHURCH so special that you chose it as your own? The church you attend today was planted by someone who cared about your neighborhood, community, and world long before you came along. God placed in the planter's spirit the heart to reach those around them with the gospel of Jesus Christ. Sadly, today the gospel is being drowned out in a sea of voices that are screaming: What about me? Me! No, me first!

Dr. Carl Summer, a retired district superintendent in the Southwest Oklahoma District wrote, "Every Church exists because somebody cared for somebody besides themselves. It seems to me that for a church to decide they are going to take care of themselves first and foremost and basically ignore those outside the walls of the Church is a violation of the very spirit that created them."[1]

The local church was not founded to be a shrine to the pastor or to the people that attend. The church was designated where it sits today to reach the lost for Christ. The voice of Christ is to help and not hinder. To love, and not judge. To extend grace, and not damnation.

Churches today have so many rules, which the rule makers become the rule breakers because they can't keep them straight. Pope Francis said in Rome in 2013, "We have fallen into globalized indifference, we have become use to the suffering of others."[2]

1. Carl Summer, email message to author, Aug 5, 2013.

2. Pope Francis, "Homily of Holy Father Francis" (Jul 8, 2013, https://www.vatican.va/content/francesco/en/homilies/2013/documents/

1

Christ suffered so that we could see the sea of humanity that needed saving. He suffered so that we could be free from sin. The church you call home must be more like Christ in mindset, attitude, and above all, heart. The voice of the underprivileged must be heard. The voice of the lost must be allowed to cry and to be comforted. The voice of the hurting must be healed through love, friendship, and compassion.

Christ is calling the local church to pick up its fellow man and love him as Christ loves his church. To see the sinner, not as a sinner, but a name and face. To respond compassionately with love and not judgement on the plight of others.

The church you call home must have faith that overrides emotional reactions, in seeing the spirit led life that a person could be, and not what the person is today. What was meant for harm by the world can be transformed through the love of the local church people that shows kindness, grace, and above all the heart of Christ, through servanthood.

The mission of local church and the global big "C" church is living out Christlikeness not just on Sundays, but every day of the week. Take up the challenge to "be the church," and serve the neighborhood around your church and the community. The call that permeates the pages of this book is to recapture the service heart of the local church to go and reach the neighborhood and the city with gospel.

You are called. You are able. Will you go?

Dr. Desmond Barrett and Dr. Charlotte P. Holter

papa-francesco_20130708_omelia-lampedusa.html).

# Chapter 1

## Living on Mission
### Developing a Missional Mindset

WALKING INTO THE FELLOWSHIP hall, a mid-twenty-year-old convert to Christianity did not know what to expect. All he knew was that he was called upon, maybe even drafted, if he were honest, to help decorate the fellowship hall for a Faith Promise dinner that was coming the following weekend. The dinner theme would transport church members to a different place and time while speaking to their hearts about God calling them to sow into missions. For a recent convert to the faith, Faith Promise was a relatively obscure name for a meal that would drive missions home in the hearts of those who would be attending, he thought. As he opened the door, Judy was busy pulling things out of boxes and bags that she had brought with her. Her heart for living on a mission for Christ would direct her to dedicate forty years of her life to cleaning the church as a love offering to God, but here she was as the local mission's president, preparing the church for a memorable weekend.

The young man could barely get the word "hello" out of his mouth before she began directing him to move this table, put that object here, and move this one there. When it was all done, they both marveled at how fast this small team took in decorating a somewhat outdated fellowship hall and turning it into a world marketplace where the dinner theme came alive through decorations, flags, and place settings. The stage was set for a dinner that would impact many and raise awareness for the cause of missions.

As the room filled with church members, excitement for the night's event was felt by all who gathered. The aroma from the awaiting food rolled out of the small kitchen that adjoined the fellowship hall and enticed the guests about what was to come. Music played softly in the background to draw the guests' ears to an imaginary ocean-front villa and helped set the scene for what was to come. As dinner was served, the chatter in the room raised to a volume heard at local restaurants as people talked about the delicious food and the festive atmosphere the room had provided. The guest missionary and family held court as they mingled amongst the tables and began even by their very presence to transport the crowd to their service area in the global church. That night the people fully understood that missions are not about getting but about giving all; they had to support the work of Jesus around the world.

That was the first of many Faith Promise weekends where the young man, now a pastor, saw God move in the hearts of the church. Reflecting upon that night, he remarked how the people were on fire for what God was doing around the world as the world came to them in the fellowship hall. The people that weekend were willing to give of their resources to invest in missions and do it with joy. If that night was the pinnacle, the valley awaited them; as the excitement of the Faith Promise weekend dissipated over time, the people allowed themselves to be lolled back into their slumber.

"Taking" rather than "giving" inside the church ensued. In seeing this example played out in this local church and subsequent churches, the soon-to-be pastor observed, "What happens to the local church when members define missions as a one-and-done yearly event?" That question spoken as an afterthought in the conversation has grown roots and struck a nerve in our imaginations as we have been unable to shake that conversation.

As we ponder the question on a broader scale, if the church is to be effective, it must be a church living on a mission. Is living on missions just for Bible days? Can missions be for the church in the twenty-first century? In surveying the current times we live in, is society so self-absorbed and unable to balance missions and meaning? Could the church pull itself away from the social media debates to focus on the needs around them? We think yes. Why? Because we have seen churches that turn from selfish ways toward the saviors, restoring the church's heartbeat. Dr. Nina Gunter, a former general superintendent in the Church of the Nazarene, shared, "The Church is not in crisis. As the Church is in Christ."[1] If you believe as we do in the statement, where is the church today?

While the North American church may look like it is in crisis, there is a remnant of believers, like you, who have stayed in Christ and are restoring the church and her surroundings by living like Jesus and serving on mission. Neighborhoods and cities around many of her churches are decaying, dying, and souls are going to hell. All the while, the church remains quiet.

## RESHAPING THE MISSIONAL VISION

Far too many churches in North America are either plateauing or dying. In almost every community, a former church is either closed or turned into something other than who she used to be. It is heartbreaking to see where once people glorified God, today, he has been sold away as the church property, changed hands through a sale, or auctioned on the courthouse steps. One must realize that it is not one decision that closed the established church but multiple decisions sometimes made over decades that got it to closure. Without a clear mission, the church lurched inward and slowly died. One does not have to look very far to find the missional call found in Matthew (28:16–20) or, as others call it, the "Great Commission." Yet where is the church on mission today? Far too many are focused on internal matters instead of external spiritual issues and are allowing millions to go to hell without knowing the redeeming grace of Jesus Christ.

1. Nina Gunter, "Good News for the Church" (n.d., https://www.preachersmagazine.org/good-news-for-the-church/).

What will it take for a transformation to happen? Missional service will take a willing heart to serve others locally and internationally as the hands and feet of Christ. It will take the ability to keep learning and growing in God's grace while celebrating victories as they come. It seems basic, right? Yet, most churches in communities like yours do not support missionaries through programs tied to mission agencies or investing locally to reach the lost. The time of inaction has lapsed, and it is time for God's church to come alive through visionary local leadership to promote and then lead in the area of missions.

## Create a Vision for the People to Capture

What do you see each day as you drive to work or go shopping? For many, they see the car in front of them, ignoring the neighborhood blight and the plight of the man standing on the street corner holding up a sign asking for food. When you take off the rosy glasses of economic class, you will begin to see the streets as they are. Businesses shuttered, abandoned homes, and overall financial distress. But, where others may see misery, the church should see it as an opportunity to live on a mission, like Jesus, to the hurting and broken world. While Jesus cast the vision for the church and its members to serve, it takes the leadership of a local pastor or the mission-oriented heart of a lay member to begin to cast a wider net.

One of the first things new pastors usually change when they come to a church is the mission statement. Think for a moment about what the local church's mission statement is. If the mission statement is biblically-based, why do pastors need to change it? If it's for preference, then it should probably be left alone. If it's too long, more than a sentence, maybe it could be shortened but not eliminated. How many times have you looked at the church's mission statement? Probably not a lot. Instead of dismissing it, embrace the mission statement and use it as a launching pad for creating and casting the vision for the people to capture. The mission statement needs to be clear, concise, and community-focused or the congregation will not embrace the concept or act it out in their daily lives.


## Create Opportunities to Serve Locally and Globally

At the turn of the century, the church looked culturally and religiously different than it does today. Some may say thank goodness, while others dread the dark ages the church has entered in their estimation. Yet through it all, the message of Christ has not changed. While churches have adapted to the changing cultures to reach the lost with the gospel in new ways, the message has not changed. What has changed is the wants and desires of the people in the pews. In yesteryear, missions came to the people in dedicated missions or deputation services. Today, people want to be on a mission wherever they go, not just once a month or year. While previous generations wanted to fund missions through giving, today's generation wants to give through service in the field. As this shift takes place within the local church, the church needs to partner with the community in achieving the results if they are going to expand the kingdom. Instead of the church navigating the new waters with pessimism, the people need to shift to become optimistic. Optimistic about serving hands-on and not just writing a check or attending a service.

In every community, agencies and nonprofit organizations desperately need volunteers and financial support. While many churchgoers have dreamt about serving on the foreign mission field, many do not get to live out their dream. Instead of losing the vision, the local church can be a sending agency that invests in the community. The goal (of expanding the kingdom) can be achieved by contextualizing the community's needs around them. Local neighborhoods need missionaries to serve, and pockets of communities are waiting for missionaries from the church to connect to the opportunities across town or in the next-door county.

The North American church has incredible wealth compared to the big "C" churches worldwide. Serving locally does not have to be at the expense of investing in world missions, as members can help locally and support internationally. There are endless possibilities to help others as the hands and feet of Christ if the church is willing to move from an inside looking posture to an outward service posture.

Investing internationally or locally through resources (prayers, people, and financial means) helps grow the church, where many North American members will never go. Christ needs the church, and the church needs to see Christ's vision as they sow generously through their time, talent, and treasure at home and around the world.

## Create Celebration Days

As you have read the words above, maybe your heart has been stirred to become the missionary God has created you to be. With today's technology, the world is not thousands of miles away but in the palm of your hand through your cell phone, which has enabled the world to grow smaller. While you may never reach the foreign mission field, you can make a lasting impact at home and internationally if you are willing to celebrate where God is and what God is doing. By telling others how God is using you to impact the needs around you, you begin to have the missional zeal of winning the lost. Use the technology in your hands to create opportunities to serve the global church from the comfort of your living room or the church fellowship hall. Invite missionaries to connect with the local church through Zoom services and conversations. As the church speaks with missionaries and learns about the plight around the world, they are more likely to want to invest. Celebrate days like this, where God brings home these missional connections between the foreign and home fields.

*Celebrate where God is*: Where is God already moving in the community around the church? That is where God may want you to connect. Give of yourself and invest in a local nonprofit, soup kitchen, pregnancy center, or where you see God already at work. Invest your resources and that of the church's, and tell others about what God is doing through the church. In the celebration moments, God is lifted high, and spirits are open to receiving the call on their own lives.

*Celebrate what God is doing:* The work you do for the Lord is far more critical than a sporting franchise victory, yet people are more apt at celebrating a winning score of their favorite sports team than celebrating a soul won for Christ. The local church's work should be celebrated at every vantage point. When the church celebrates a God win, they redeem what was lost for God's good. Celebrating reminds those still on the sidelines of service that God is up to something, and they should join in.

*Celebrate how God is transforming you:* When you invest as a local or international missionary, you invest where God is. Serving others is more about changing you than transforming the lives around you. Sure, people and organizations benefit from the hours you serve or funds invested, but the person giving gets the added benefit of becoming a new creation in Christ. That is when we believe the angels of heaven celebrate.

A life transformed from the mundane to living on a mission should be celebrated at each turning point. Celebrate how God is using you personally with others. Share your story with the church or with strangers, but whatever you do, share. God can use your story of transformation to transform lives around the community if you are willing to speak up.

Think about it this way, shaping the vision of missions from the pulpit to the pew is all about living a life surrendered to God's will. You do not have to have a theology degree to serve, but you do need an understanding that God has formed you for something far more significant than who you think or imagine you could be.

## MOVING FROM THE MUNDANE INTO A MISSIONARY JOURNEY

As the ball dropped in Times Square on New Year's Eve 2019, the world looked on with anticipation for a new decade and year ahead. A pandemic, political polarization, and a populace split splintered the hopes and dreams of many with a bang. With the advent of 2020, the clarity that many longed for became clouded through the fog of world happenings. As major cities erupted in riots and protests related to police brutality and differences stoked by political and community leaders, where was the church? Many were forced to close for months, and restrictive mask mandates seemed to choke out the presence of God as churches labored to find common ground amongst all the turmoil. In this season of darkness, God's light began to shine brighter, and the church began to find hope again.

As the world outside the church walls began to groan with differences, the church awakened to the needs around them. She began to see the need to connect more deeply with each other and the community crying out for help. Far too many churches had become social clubs that maintained the workings of the church to fit their best interest rather than the neighborhood around the church property. As the numbers inside began to wane, the church began to change. This uncertain season of strife forced the church to look outside at the needs around them. The crisis that pounded like a beating drum against the psyche of the church's soul could not be ignored any longer. A change had come to the community of faith, and the question had been asked: Was the church willing to change or adapt its mission to reach the broken community around them or ignore the plight and slowly die from a lack of attendance?

It would only be through the guidance of the Holy Spirit that the church would reconnect to the community in such a transformational and missional way that would help save them (the community and church) both.


## The Promise of Expanding the Kingdom into the Wider Community

As the world seemed to be cratering into a social-civil war, the local church had a choice. To either join the fight for whatever side they felt pulled towards or see Christ amid the darkness. For the missional-focused church, she sought the broader mission of

Christ and joined hands with those who were hurting. She began to love like never before the community around them. While differences were present, God guided the healing process, enabling the chasm of the sanctified nature to cover the divide where once wide gaps were laid bare for the world to see. Love can overcome many sins, and when the local church is leading out of love, they live as Great Commission people.

Outside of your church doors today is a community waiting to be embraced with the love of Christ. Explore where the community needs are located and go there. Bring what you and others have found in examining the community needs. Share them on a whiteboard. Write them on a piece of paper. Or express them in an open meeting where ideas and conversations about those needs are addressed and prayed over. You do not have to reinvent the spiritual wheel, but you do need the will to see where God is at work and go there.

As the discussions conclude, let us challenge you to keep the conversation going, so the church does not fall into missional ineffectiveness. With the mission ideas captured in these discussions, it is time to develop a plan to become missionally engaged.

## The Plan Is to Develop Every Church Attendee as a Missionary

From the pastor to the pew, everyone has the potential to be a missionary for God. We use the word "potential" because it is a choice. Sadly, many churchgoers want to attend church but do not want to live out what they are learning. While some may ignore or outright reject the call on their lives, as a leader in the church, you should develop a workable plan to share the vision, design training, then activate and deploy the missionary forces into the community. As we believe, everyone is a called missionary, and if you do not answer the call, that disobedience must grieve God.

*Share the vision:*

1. Consider the specific needs that the church desires to focus on within the community.

2. Find three to six nonprofit agencies that are diverse in what they do and need volunteers.

3. Once those partnerships are secured, have a night where each of the agencies attends to share with your lay missionaries to learn firsthand the needs, what they might be doing, and how their investment will make a difference.

*Develop training:*

1. Set up training times as your lay missionaries express a willingness to invest time with a particular agency.

2. The outside agency should handle these training times and include fellowship, team building, and knowledge-skill building to encourage a strong working relationship between the lay missionary and the community agency.

*Activate missionary forces:*

1. The Sunday morning before the lay missionaries enter the community, host a sending service to celebrate what God is getting ready to do through the church. Think about bringing in a special speaker who will challenge everyone in the congregation to step out of their comfort zone and be Jesus in the community.

2. Pray over the team members.

3. Host a celebratory dinner on the grounds. Find creative ways to decorate through international flags, special music, and sharing food from around the world.

While your lay missionaries will not be traveling far, use the sending service to send a subtle message to your church members that the church is invested in others locally and around the world.

God is moving in the life of the church and her community today. When the church comes outside her walls and begins to serve the community like never before, lives are changed, and the community will become better for it.

## MISSIONAL MOMENTS:

1. Where is God at work in the community and how can the local church partner?

2. How is the church celebrating "God's victories" that are found in missional advancement?

3. What is the simulation plan to identify, equip, and send local missionaries into the community?

# Chapter 2

# Growing Disciple Makers from Within

HAVE YOU WATCHED OR participated in a race, and you've heard the words, "Ready. Set. Go"? If you have, then you know the excitement and maybe even nervous anticipation for the race about to start. Once the flag or starting whistle has blown, you realize that you are all alone quickly. Sure, there are others around you on the course or on the sidelines cheering the group on, but you essentially are alone inside your thoughts—all the training, special dieting, and exercising were for this moment. The race will not be won or lost by what you did in the past, but by course conditions. You can control course conditions as you experience the highs and lows of the race by focusing on yourself, not others around you. All the training in the world would not change how you react to the conditions you face on the course, as you have to live in the moment. So, too, for the established church when it comes to missions. The church you serve in today was most likely planted decades ago with a missional seed to reach a community or neighborhood with the gospel of Christ. That seed germinated in the hearts of others. The early planters and converts tended to the faith they had. So, what happened? Why are so many churches plateauing or declining and have lost their focus on helping others?

Somewhere along the course of the race, the people veered off God's missional vision for the church. Maybe a pit stop happened during a pastoral transition. A pull-up occurred during infighting between the members. Whatever the cause, the race that started so strong has become a struggle. All the goodwill planted early on in the hearts of the planters has dissipated over time. Now the church is just trying to hold on. When a church faces a crisis of identity, they either double down on what they are doing wrong, think it is correct, or begin anew in a new direction. In all reality, the record of achievement will only be known in the church that lives or dies, and even then, eternity will be the reaper of the fruit.

So ask yourself: Will my local church change or keep doing the same thing expecting different results? Will I serve out my calling as a local missionary? Will I help the church live or let them die?

## FIND THE CHURCH'S PURPOSE

Walking the halls of your church, what do you sense is the purpose of your church? To help members with their needs? Serve in the community? Reach the lost? Share the gospel? Somewhere inside the hallowed halls is the answer. Ask yourself again: What is the purpose of my local church?

Plaques, trophies, and other hardware show the visitor what she used to be, but today the established church is bleeding members, aging as a population, and has lost most of its missional zeal. But that does not have to be the ending point. Use the negative feeling as a warning sign to change and adapt to the demographics and needs currently experienced by the community just steps from the steeple of your church.

The church cannot go into the community as lay missionaries until it knows "why" it should go in the first place. Regardless if you are a pastor or a lay member of the church, you should begin to evaluate, observe, and talk about who the church is today and where you want her to be in the future. Conversations will lead to conversions down the road if the church is willing to find its purpose.

## Find the Church's Passion

So, what is your local church's passion? While just a building, the church consists of wonderful, passionate Jesus followers like you. What you are passionate about will be lived out by your excitement, focus, and acknowledgment. There are things that the church people are passionate about that have to be delineated. Sometimes passion is seen in tradition, dedicated rooms, or special nameplates on furniture. Other times passion is seen in collecting things that fill up former classrooms where children once played. Whatever the church's current emphasis, it should be evaluated for gospel effectiveness.

Instead of the passion being for things, God wants the passion for winning the lost, disciplining the multitude, and walking in obedience with him. Derive the desire from what is attainable and use it in your local context. For instance, you may see a homeless person on a street corner or asleep in your downtown area, and you know the local community kitchen needs volunteers. You can take your knowledge of the problem and combine it with your passion for serving others and use it as the hands and feet of Jesus in helping the homeless. It does not take a lot of money or time to be effective. On the other hand, it does take a passion for propelling the church forward into the community.

## Find the Church's Position

For many established churches, they are shells of their former glory. They have a large building but a small footprint compared to the average weekly attendance. With the average size of the church smaller today than it was ten years ago, the church cannot do what it did in the past. Simply replicating the former glory days will not help the church's turnaround. It will instead quicken the pace toward closure.

While the position of the past does not dictate the missional health of the church today, you can use it to lay a strong foundation for future missional outreach. The community does not need nor want the grand, glorious buildings or programs of the past, but a people who will accept the unacceptable, care for the aging, and love orphans of the community. Using limited resources the church has in a narrowly focused way can meet the community's needs through a missional church. God can use your excuse (we don't have people or money) and turn it into an exercise of faith when you partner with God.

While the church may feel winded by the race she's running up to this point, the church still has more in her tank to give. This leg of the church's journey is not an ending or even a detour from the missional call, but we see it as a portion of the race where all the past training will pay off, and with your help, God will take the church to the finish line.

## DEVELOPING LAY MISSIONARIES FOR KINGDOM ADVANCEMENT

For many established churches, the only time they hear about a missionary is during a special missionary visit or when the pastor wants to take an offering for an organization in the community. Living on a mission is living out one's faith daily. Not once a year or during a particular offering time. As you think about your calling, trace your mind back to the first time you met Jesus. Maybe it was as a child or a grown adult. Reflect on that feeling. Remember who called you and why you accepted the invitation made by God. That day must have been exhilarating. The sentiment you experienced then is the moment that God is calling you and the church back to now. God has identified you as one of his. He has called you for such a time as this. In this season of your ministry, he is asking you to recharge your spiritual batteries and begin a new season of work for the greater kingdom. Are you willing? Because God knows you are able. Is the church ready? Because God knows she is needed. When you say, "yes," God will open the flood gates of heaven and pour out his blessing for kingdom advancement like never before.

## Identify Who Feels Called

No one feels called or even adequate for what God asks them to do. Many churches and her people have not lived out their true calling because they have allowed self-doubt to creep in and take hold of God's calling on their lives. God has not given up and is still calling his church. Leaders have a unique vantage point in the church to see people's giftings long before they see their own. Through this identification process, a leader obeys the direction of the Holy Spirit and begins to host conversations with potential lay missionaries to reach the community around them.

These conversations should be bathed in prayer, be focused on the need to serve others, and have a heart for the mission field outside the church's campus. Allow God to direct you to a person(s) inside the church that can help expand the kingdom footprint of the church.

## Identify Who Has Giftings

As you have been praying for God's direction, we believe that he will open your eyes to see the kingdom-makers in front of you. When you observe the people in your church, what do you see? We are not speaking of the physical appearance of someone, but the spiritual giftings that God has placed inside of them. Each person sitting in the pew has giftings that God needs to help make the community noticeably better. In personal one-on-one interactions or even in a large class where you lead the class through the "spiritual gifts inventory," you can help encourage, point out, and speak about the giftings that a person may not even realize they have.

Christians today live in a social media-driven society where every post is captured through the lens of a filter and not reality.

The outside scroller evaluates their own lives in comparison and struggles with their self-worth. This negative image thought process has filtered into the local church. Christians with great giftedness do not see or use their giftings for the kingdom because they have a different picture of their abilities and where God can use them. That is where you come in as a leader. You can call out and direct a member's view to see where God has placed a spiritual seed. You can encourage that God seed through a fostering of discipleship over time.

## Identify Who Needs Development

Throughout the Scriptures, you can read stories of lives transformed through intentional discipleship between believers. Sadly, disciple-making is not a priority for many churches in North America today. Dr. Jerry Porter, a retired general superintendent in the Church of the Nazarene, was fond of asking, "Who is discipling you? Who are you discipling? Who is the disciple, discipling?" This biblical discipleship model is not new. It has been around for centuries, and Jesus was the best-known teacher for the established church to follow.

Jesus identified people and positions where he needed help from others, and he went out and personally talked to prospective candidates. He would intentionally develop their skill sets through one-on-one, small, and large group discipleship times. Today, this model can still be effective and duplicated by you in your local church. As a missional leader, you must recognize that you cannot develop everyone, but you can develop someone. Your one can become two, supporting consistent multiplication efforts until you reach critical mass within the church. God is calling you to equip your people, but will you obey?

## Identify Jesus in the Masses

As the people inside the church begin to catch the vision to live on mission daily, they will want to know the next step. The next step is where your leadership abilities come into play. You must have the next step ready to go, or the people will regress in their spiritual walk. Begin to share your heart for the community around the established church with your people. Listen to where they are in viewing the city for Jesus. Find commonality in that calling. Begin to prepare to go where Jesus is needed or already at work in your town. The result of serving as the hands and feet of Christ to a lost and broken world will not be easy. But it can be rewarding when you do it with the right heart.

Being a lay missionary is not always helping the ones you want to help but helping all who have fallen short of the glory of the Lord. While serving as Jesus in the community, there was a man we will call Robert. He had a troubled childhood and had committed a heinous crime against an underage child. He would spend twelve years in prison for his crimes and, once released, was put on the sex offender registry. Society has cast him aside for what he did, but Jesus brought him across our path so that we could share the "good news" with him. As we tried to look past the vial acts and sins he committed, God began to give us the eyes of Jesus to see Robert not by the world's labels but by what God called him to be, a child of his.

Ministry is not always easy. Sometimes it calls you into the gutters of the world, where you serve the undesirable as Jesus did back in his time. It can be painful and powerful simultaneously, and you must remember that it is Jesus who called you. It is Jesus who has equipped you. Jesus has identified the sinner and the saint who will restore each from their worldly slumber. When you act as a light of Christ in a darkened world, you live out your missionary call in a powerful way.

## OBEYING THE CALL ON YOUR LIFE

Your mind might be whirling from what God is asking you to do. You picked up this book to focus on missions, and now he is calling you to be the missionary to enter the mission field. We get it. You sought this book looking for practical tools to reset your missional plan for the church, but, surprise, it starts with you. God is calling you to advance the missional zeal in your local church. While you may not feel called to enter a foreign field, the field you are joining (the local community) is ripe for the harvest if you are willing to submit, commit, and admit the calling to obey. You are the "soul winner" God needs to help transform your neighborhood.

In Max Lucado's book *It's Not about Me: Rescue from the Life We Thought Would Make Us Happy*, he writes, "God lets you excel so you can make him known."[1] Inside of you is the giftings that he needs for this season in the church's life. Sure, you can point it out in others, but can you see it in yourself? God is asking you to prayerfully submit, commit, and admit to the calling on your life.

## Submit to God's Authority

As a leader, you are use to directing and guiding. But who directs and guides you? Perhaps it is a church board, denominational leadership, or a mentor? Someone is leading you, but who? The one who guides is the ultimate provider in your life. It cannot be family, fortune, or favorite things; it must be God, which takes total submission. Ultimately God wants you to submit to his authority over your life and ministry. We understand it is not easy to get to where you fully surrender your life, church, and calling. But to be effective in your missional call, you must find that vulnerable space to submit to God's authority over your life.

Before you go any further in this book, why don't you pause and reflect on where you are spiritually, physically, and emotionally

---

1. Max Lucado, *It's Not About Me: Rescue from the Life We Thought Would Make Us Happy* (Nashville: Integrity, 2004), 133.

with God. If you feel comfortable, follow this little exercise. On a piece of paper, write the following three headlines:

## SPIRITUAL SUBMISSION—PHYSICAL SUBMISSION—EMOTIONAL SUBMISSION

Under each heading, working left to right, write down the first thing that comes to mind under each category and keep repeating the exercise until you cannot think of anything else to write down. Then evaluate the list. Where do you have the most things written down? Where have you fully submitted over to God? Where have you struggled to find something to write? These categories will expose your strengths and weaknesses if you allow the Holy Spirit to guide your mind and hand. Use this exercise to help you know where God is working and where you need him to move in your spirit. This activity, while simple, is a reminder that submitting to God's authority is not a one-and-done activity but a daily act of surrender on your part. God will nurture your submission into the commission's action if you are willing.

## Commit to God's Plans

God has a divine plan for your local church and is willing to use you to bring about that plan if you commit to his will for your ministry. When we say ministry, we are not just saying ministers, but if you have the opportunity to impact someone's life, you have a ministry. So, what will it take for you to fully commit to God's plans over your life and ministry? We have seen God use three areas in our lives, and we believe he can use them to help you in your life.

- **Commit in prayer:** Each day, spend time alone with God committing your life, ministry, and calling over to him. If you pray for five minutes or five hours, listen as you pray for his direction and guidance, and then obey. Through a determined prayer life, God creates in you a new missional life that will strengthen you spiritually to lead others into the arms of the Lord.

- **Commit to preparing**: God wants a willing partner to serve with him in ministry. You and the local church are strategically positioned to reach your community with the gospel. Many want to go out and help without preparing spiritually or mentally in prayer and study. Commit to preparing by learning the needs, connecting to outside community resources, and serving in the conditions before you with a willing heart.

- **Commit to progress:** Serving in the community is not easy. Sure, it sounds easy, but you might feel overwhelmed and want to give up when you begin, as we have felt that way. Instead, do not give up; give in to God's call and not your desires. Commit now, even before you start to progress forward one day at a time, trusting God. Let us encourage you directly from our experiences not to allow the circumstances before you to dictate the call inside of you. Push through. Push yourself to be who God has created you to be.

## ADMIT YOU NEED GOD

There will be times in your ministry journey when you feel that you are all alone. That feeling of emptiness is not new. We have felt the same way many times before. Leaders at all levels have felt this longing for something greater than themselves. In this emptiness and inadequacy, you must admit you cannot do it alone. Give it to God.

Do us a favor, turn on the movie screen of your imagination for a moment: See God as a big cheerleader, cheering you and your heart for others as you serve in the community. When it gets complicated and challenging serving others in the community, we want you to picture God whispering and sometimes shouting, "Don't give up! Keep going! Almost there!"

How many times in your life have you given up just short of where God wanted you to end up on your journey? Or how many times did the church not change and miss her calling? Do not be counted out as a quitter, but as a forward-moving Christian who calls out to God, commits to his plan, and admits when you need him. Missionary leader, the neighborhood just outside your church's doors needs you and your church. Will you say "yes" to God and follow through?

## MISSIONAL MOMENTS:

1. Why is it so hard for people to get connected to missions inside and outside the local church?

2. How can the local churchchange the perception of missions?

3. Is the local church praying for missions outside of traditional times? If not, where can prayer be started and for who?

# Chapter 3

# Seeking Community Connections
## Serving the Neighborhood

YOU CAN FIND A tent city of displaced people through the undergrowth along a well-worn path about a mile outside the town limits. While their bodies were ravaged by addiction and their mental health complicated by incarceration in the past, they have found peace in this tranquil place. In conversations like these, with people labeled as undesirables by society, you can see the face of Jesus looking back at you. While the words spoken that day did not transform hearts, they propelled the actions of Christ from the church building into the streets, where Jesus is calling his church. Serving in the community might not be easy, but it is worth it as you see lives slowly transformed into the image of Christ.

Not too long ago, churches would fill up with Christ-seekers to hear the word preached, sing songs, pass the offering plate, and talk with friends. Over time things have shifted from in-person gatherings to observing the church through their social media pages. Google has become the church's new front door, songs have evolved, offerings are gathered online, and people look more at their phones than people's faces when they are out in public. Once the church held services three times a week, many churches have accelerated change by moving to one day a week services since the pandemic. In a much earlier time, the church used to be seen as a community hub. Today, she has become a social club holding on to traditions and not letting go of the past. So, where does a church go that has not adapted to the changing times of society as the message found in God's word has never changed?

## REFOCUS OUTSIDE THE WALLS

The work that God is calling the church to is not an easy place, but a place where he needs the church to refocus her eyes and energy. As the church adapts to new cultural norms, it must adjust to the missional shift within the community. Where once the church collected offerings while hearing stories from mission fields around the world, today, the area that God is calling the church to is just around the corner from their physical location. The reality is the church is no longer an island unto herself but a lighthouse of hope in a sin-filled world around her. Within feet of her front doors lies a mission field of societal decay that you and the local church need to help solve.

## Repair the Breach

How often have you driven by someone in need and ignored their plight? We all have. So instead of changing the past, begin to think about how you can help in the future. Inside your local church are people who feel called to help but do not know where to start. A friend of ours, Pastor Jane Jarrells, has a passion for helping others. Maybe it comes from her calling by God or her work with the Salvation Army, but she sees the hungry and wants to feed them. She had mentioned it a time or two to others in her church, and instantly she saw the interest and realized that the church could do something at least once a month. Assembling a team, she encouraged members to donate funds, and in turn, the team used those funds by putting their love of cooking and their love of service to work. By observing the need in her community, Pastor Jane has led a small but mighty revolution to feed homeless people once a month in partnership with another nonprofit. Her courageous act of action has changed lives. She changed the lives of the people she provides food for and the members who serve alongside her. What about you? What is the one act that God has been calling you to do, but you have not had the courage? Where is the area in your community where the church could repair the breach and solve a problem? God is waiting; are you willing?

## Restore the Calling

Throughout the community, social service agencies need volunteers to help fill in the gaps where funding has decreased, but the conditions have increased. A local community kitchen in town has lost 85 percent of its volunteers during the pandemic, but the number of meals served has stayed steady. Volunteers are desperately needed to help lessen the burden on an already overstretched staff. Could your church help? How about that clothing center that collects clothing for needy individuals and families? Could you help collect clothes or sort them at a processing center for them? There are hundreds of projects in your community that need you and your church. Our one caution would be not to stretch yourself too thin, trying to do too much too soon. Find a project or two and commit to becoming long-term sponsors of the projects and restore God's call on your church's life to connect with the community.

## WIN ONE FOR JESUS

It can be overwhelming when you begin to hear God's voice to enter the harvest field and live out your faith in ministry. Take heart that God has called and commissioned you to be the local missionary to win the harvest, one person at a time. Take a deep spiritual breath and realize the mandate that you follow is not to win the nearly eight billion people in the world but the one person in front of you. That means you are off the spiritual hook for 7,999,999,999 other people. Your calling is to win the one in front of you, one conversation and action at a time. Maybe you are asking, well, how? Glad you asked. It would help if you had practical missional approaches to reaching the lost in your community. Let us give you three easy steps to follow.

## Meet and Greet

Each day as you arise, begin to ask God in your prayer language (however and wherever you pray) to enable you to see with eyes like his. If you believe, as we do, that God has a plan for your life, then begin to call out that plan by preparing your spirit early each day to connect with the person or persons that God will bring across your path. When you pray for God appointments, be ready to be put in uncomfortable situations. God will never ask you to do anything outside of his will, but it might be outside your comfort zone. The most important aspect of praying bold prayers is to do it with sincerity of spirit, or you will miss the will of God.

As you go about your day, be open to speaking to people that do not look or act like you. When you get nervous before speaking with someone, pause and picture Jesus before you and not the guy with blue hair, tattoos, and piercings behind the cash register. As you begin to meet with God appointments that he has lined up for your new ministry as a missionary, begin to greet folks with a sincerity that comes through knowing God. Marvel as you go through short interactions and listen for the God tones you can share back with your newfound friend. You will be surprised at how easy it will become to share your faith by living it out in coffee shops, grocery store lines, and daily routines.

Recently as we were having lunch, the waitress across the room was passing out receipts for the meal to customers that she had served. As she said her goodbyes, she asked, "Do you have a church home?" If the customers said yes, she would encourage them to show up to their local church weekly and pray for their pastor. If they said no, she would invite them to her church. It was a magnificent display of the meet-and-greet philosophy of living out one's faith. Living as a missionary will not be easy, but it can be rewarding with one conversation that can lead over time to conversion.

## Live and Learn

As you get more comfortable in tuned with God's guidance, you will have more opportunities to move from superficial interactions to deep spiritual connections. These connections may bloom into friendships or acquaintances, but see them as God moments you can use to live and learn with your God connection. Today, you live in a world so interconnected that many have become disconnected in sharing basic life with someone other than immediate family. Even the family unit has broken down because everyone has their head in their phones. The computer age has allowed the world to communicate through emojis, 280-characters on Twitter, or a one-minute video on TikTok, which has caused people to feel uncomfortable sharing a basic conversation over the phone or in person.

As a local missionary, you can live life over an extended period with people out in the community. During these long-term assignments, you can learn more about a person, their family, needs, and hopes for the future. One thing that you can learn from long-term missionaries on the field in global areas is that relationships are hard to build up but easy to lose if you do not take the time to build a strong foundation with a person. Living and learning on a mission use basic conversations to build trust and understanding with the one God has sent you to connect with over time. Spend God moments not in a rush but reassuring your friend that you care about their story and want to invest long-term in the relationship. This approach will bear fruit if you are passionate about serving others while patient enough to allow the relationship to develop in God's timing.

## Share and Dare

As you get to know your "new" friend better, they will permit you to speak into their life. In this season of share and dare, you can win or lose your newfound convert. If it sounds like a lot of responsibility, it is. Sharing your faith can be tricky in a hypertensive world that pushes back against anything that smells and looks like old-fashioned religion. Sadly, too many people have experienced hurt in the church, which causes one not to want to go back down that path again. As a missionary, you must permit them to feel that way and not judge them. In this backdrop, you should help heal those wounds through the actions and words of Jesus that you will be modeling. By then, you would have spent the time to develop a deeper understanding of who they are and what life experiences have guided them. In this relationship season, you can begin to share all spiritual aspects of your own life more deeply with them. The keyword to understand is "own." When you share your own story, a person is more apt to find a piece of your account that relates to their own lives and thus, share in return. That is when God begins to dare you to share about him in more detail. This stage is long-term and does not happen quickly, so do not rush it. Be spiritually strategic as you lean into their story to share the Christ story.

Be ready for acceptance and rejection when you share the God transformation that could happen in their lives. Some will embrace a relationship with God, while others will reject it, but remember this truth, you have done what God has called you to do. Acceptance or rejection is on the person you shared your faith with, and trust the Holy Spirit to guide their heart.

## COMMUNAL NEIGHBORHOODS

Think back to your childhood. If you are of a certain age, you can remember long summer days spent outside, freely playing with your neighbors, running to a friend's house for a drink or a quick snack before your parents called you home for a family meal. The days of letting children play outside unattended have dissipated in many communities. So, can your local community ever get back to communal neighborhoods where neighbors watched out for each other and shared meals? We believe so. With Jesus, all things are possible.

We imagine you have heard the saying that "the church is not a building. The people are the church." We do not know who said it, but boy, have we heard it repeatedly in churches that needed to reset their missional identity. We understand. The established church is not a building, but the community does not see the nuance. The neighborhood recognizes the church as a building with a physical address. The campus of your church represents to many the established church. Sure, the church is made up of community members, but many in the community do not feel welcomed even if the church sign says "All Are Welcomed." As the established church struggled to rebound from a penchant for looking inward over the last few decades, she has faced difficulties building a bridge with her neighbors. But, as you have read already, not all is lost. God has a plan for the church, and that plan is you. As a missionary, you can help the church reconnect with the community by developing neighborhood prayer centers that focus on people and projects.

## Neighborhood Prayer Centers

In the heart of our urban centers, you see violence on a scale not seen outside of war. There is a rampant opioid crisis in our rural communities that is taking a staggering number of lives daily, and what do these two vastly different areas desperately need? More Jesus! While many of these communities have multiple churches of all denominations and faiths, the communities are still struggling in sin. Why? Because they need more Jesus, which can only come through prayer power. But does Jesus have the missionary support to help lead a prayer revolution? Are you the one, or is your church?

A mighty move of God comes upon a community when desperate people pray for renewal. Your church can be the prayer center that sparks revival in your neighborhood and city. Will you pray? Will you lead prayer gatherings? The Bible does not constitute prayer just for the pastor but for all to seek the face of God. Join together in small or large groups and begin to pray for God's direction for your life and ministry.

## Neighborhood People

In a desperate world that longs for authentic relationships, the church can be a catalyst for reconnecting the community. The neighborhood around many churches has become fragmented with political and social divisions. Where once neighbors helped neighbors, now neighbors stay to themselves, and what an opportunity to heal the divide through Jesus. Neighborhood churches have a unique space to host block parties and holiday-themed events by opening their campus to other small or large community-style possibilities.

Think about the incredible gift of serving in a place where God brings families and individuals right up to the campus doorstep. Begin to see the people in the neighborhood around the church as the church's first mission field. Then shift that thinking into action and begin serving them like never before and watch how they respond over time to the faithfulness of the Father's house loving them.

## Neighborhood Projects

In every neighborhood, projects are waiting, longing for some one or group to take up their cause from playgrounds to weeding yards, or picking up trash on city streets. Know this truth, while it may seem like these projects are low-hanging fruit, they can be used as a spark to invite renewal and interest from the congregation and community in each other's activities.

Realize that it does not have to be a big project to gain maximum impact, but it does have to be a project where the church enters the mission field and shows the community the love of Christ.

Let us encourage you to take a walk with your leadership team and begin to observe the neighborhood around you at a slowdown pace. Take this walk several times before you settle on a project. With all your hearts and minds in one accord, begin to see the needs fresh and anew that a church/community partnership could bring forth. As you get back from your walk the second or even third time, begin to brainstorm ideas. Remember, no thought or project is out of bounds. Do not worry about money or a workforce, as God will provide. Trust the process. Do the work and watch the blessing come from it.

In the shadow of the church steeple, a neighborhood is waiting to reconnect with Jesus. Not through a worship service but missionary service, as your people leave the pew and enter the streets to be a living example of the hands and feet of Jesus.

## MISSIONAL MOMENTS:

1. Who is my ONE? Who is the ONE that needs to be led to the Lord?

2. Where are opportunities to serve inside and outside the church and how is that being shared with others?

3. What are some of the barriers that are keeping the local church from reaching the community and how can they be taken down and replaced with service?

# Chapter 4

# Embracing a Windshield Community View

## Long-Term Partnerships

IN THE OPENING CHAPTERS, we have taken you from the pew to outside the four walls of the church. However, we would be remiss if we did not spend some time reviewing the call to the world-areas outside of your local community. Whatever form of modern media you use to read or listen to the news, you realize that the world faces great turmoil. With turmoil happening around you, see it as an opportunity to see the world through God's eyes and become the hands and feet of Christ to a world living in strife. There is an opportunity to reach the world with the gospel in new ways with great care if you are willing to see the need. Sometimes God calls the church to serve locally or globally with its resources, and always to help. Pause, and think about it this way. As you drive down the street, you quickly notice the expansive view you have before you. The large windshield has been designed for safety and to provide the driver with a picture of the road ahead.

But on the other hand, when you back up, you have a small rearview mirror or a camera that provides a smaller view of what is behind you. Churches have used their rearview mirror as the front windshield for far too long. This smaller view of missions has failed them by not obtaining the God view that he had for their church. God calls the church to move from a rearview view to embracing a windshield worldview.

When a missionary visits your local church, they entice your mind with the sights and smells of a far-off place where Jesus is at work. From standing in a thatched hut with dirt floors to eating camel for dinner while sharing the gospel with a new convert, the call to global missions can seem exotic. From ports of call halfway around the world to living on mission in your local context, the missional call extended to every person who knows Jesus is to share Jesus with others. Every evangelical denomination has taken up this mantle to share the gospel with unreached people groups worldwide. The misnomer that someone else or another church will equip the field and spread the gospel is a falsity that needs to be removed through your local church's participation. There are people and whole countries that require you to help share the gospel. Today, the church's challenge is the challenge to reach the lost at all costs. Today, your church's challenge is to be a willing partner addressing the gap. With each church doing its part, the evangelical church can help depopulate hell, but first, you must do your part in sending the gospel around the world through your local church.

## ONE-AND-DONE MISSION PROJECTS VS. LONG-TERM IMPACT

Throughout scripture, you can read about ordinary people who live extraordinary lives by saying "yes" to God. The God of the Bible is still the God of today who is calling you and the church back into the streets and across the world to serve him. What a gift to know that God still calls, and he might be calling you as you read this book.

God has given the church two ways to serve on mission in the calling of individuals and churches as local and global missionaries. While you might never get the title from a denomination as "missionary," we are deputizing you as such, as you serve locally or globally on behalf of the church and God. Let us briefly look at two ways to serve as a missionary through local or global projects.

You might ask: What is the most effective model to entice local church members to fall in love with missions? The answer is it depends. If you have ever gone on a short or long-term mission trip, you know the benefits of either. The excitement as you prepare to travel. The anticipation in what you will do as you serve. The reflection as you begin to dream again about going back to the field. Therein lies the win for Jesus and your local church. A win for missions and a win for your soul opening to the engagement that comes through missions. While we do not advocate for one over the other (one-and-done or long-term missional service), we wanted to describe the benefits of missions briefly. Let us review short and long-term models and reflect on which one is best for you and your faith community.

## One-and-Done Mission Model

The easiest and most cost-effective way to live on missions is to serve locally or internationally on one-and-done mission trips. We define the one-and-done mission model as a short investment of time and resources in a field. This project model is targeted in time and scope and usually has the team come to the country or area once and never return.

In local areas of service, this model can be seen in community activities such as an Angel Tree giveaway at Christmas time or in global areas traveling to a foreign country for a weeklong mission trip, to work on a project but not return. These missional experiences expose faith communities to the broader need for service to and in the kingdom and are usually more affordable and take less time away from home for those attending the trip.

## Long-Term Mission Model

We define long-term mission trips as a long-term investment of time and resources in a world area that lasts over an extended period. This type of missional outreach exposes the individual and church to deeper relationships and enables investments that can make a kingdom difference over the years rather than weeks. Long-term missional engagement locally can be seen through strategic community partnerships with a homeless shelter or by adopting a village across the globe—each time returning to invest in the people and the church.

While there is justification for one-and-done trips, we have found that strategic long-term collaborative partnerships are the most effective way to do ministry. That takes vision from people/community and provides an understanding of the efforts that God has called the church to serve alongside over a prolonged period. While we celebrate exposure to missions in any way, these short-term trips lose strategic partnerships as the distance from the trip takes hold of the participants. Long-term or prolonged investment in a local or international area is desired for gospel effectiveness.

## OPEN THE GOD DOOR BEFORE YOU

As a pastor and missionary sat around talking after a deputation service, God began to move on their hearts. For two hours, the Holy Spirit began to open doors of opportunity for the local church that planted seeds for future ministry and missionary connections. As the missionary was leaving and the pastor turned the lights off, the missionary stopped and said, "someday we will do something big together for God." The pastor thought that the missionary's words were nice but would not come to pass. But God had other plans. Less than six months later, the missionary's words would ring true in the pastor's ear, as the pastor would become the head of the district's mission department. The conversation that God had planted months before took root as it moved to the forefront of the pastor's mind. God opened the doors that moved words to action. Over the next two years, the pastor would lead his denominational district to adopt a field and invest over $100,000 of resources into multiply projects. As the original participants shifted into new roles, God used the partnership to grow deeper roots and bear fresh fruit under different leaders.

How did a missionary and pastor impact the kingdom in such a big way through one conversation? The simple answer is God. By listening to God, investing in prayer, and following the Holy Spirits' prompt, lives changed for the better. What was the difference? A willingness by Christ-followers to invest long-term in a specific area. That investment has radically changed lives. So, let us ask it this way, are you willing to have God conversations? Maybe you have read the story and said, "I cannot travel abroad," but are you ready to do something closer to home. Is your soul open to God's call on your life or your church?

Pastor Steve Leppert is a New York transplant to Cordova, Alaska. When he arrived on the island that is only assessable by boat or plane, he was a fish out of water seven years ago. One would not be presumptuous to ask, how could a New Yorker impact an Alaska village? The simple answer is living like Jesus. For years Pastor Steve would dedicate himself to helping when or wherever needed. He developed a strong relationship with the Salvation Army, passing out food, clothing, and other accessories, which enabled him to become the community pastor. In the winter of 2022, he was named Cordova citizen of the year at the Iceworm Festival. *The Cordova Times*, the community paper of record, shared paragraph after paragraph of community members speaking about his leadership and love for others. So, what is the difference between Pastor Steve and you? Nothing. If you are willing, God will open the door for you to serve.

## UNLOCKING THE GOD DOOR

In a world so divided by politics and personal division, God has created a way to reach people who do not look or act like you, called missional engagement. God has provided the church with three keys to unlocking the God door before her if the church is willing to move from the pew to the streets to serve. Missional engagement is seeing a need and developing partnerships that enhance the name of Christ in the community or area that the church is investing.

## Engage the Mission Field

As your heart becomes warm to the needs of the local church and world, begin to pray singularly and corporately for God's divine guidance to lead you to an organization or field that he wants the local church to serve. For some, that will be across town, but for others, it will be in a far-off place as people are longing to hear the gospel preached, observed, and lived out. Pastor Steve's heart warmed to serve others over four thousand miles from his home. As he pondered and prayed, he knew the spirit was leading him to Cordova, Alaska, from his home in New York state. By intentionality seeking God, God changed his ministry address and thus the lives of others across the continent.

The mission fields are waiting for missionaries like you. Investors like your church in God's kingdom expansion. And prayer warriors like those who kneel at the altars each Sunday to glean the fields for Jesus. Where is your mission field that God is calling you to serve? Where is the Spirit leading you to invest the latter days of your life? It will look different for everyone and the church, but the call is the same.

## Equip the Saints

Who is it that led you to the Lord? Who are you leading to the Lord? Inside of you is a God-called charge to make disciples, who make disciples. The local church is charged with equipping leaders to become missionaries to the local and global community. For the local church, it can be the role of the pastor and local mission society inside the church to share opportunities. But someone needs to lead this charge and do it with a heart to share Jesus with others. Equipping the saints is not about gospel preaching techniques but about providing tools for future evangelism. These tools are as essential as narrowing the focus to serve, opportunities to serve, observing where to help, and mirroring evangelism techniques to share the gospel lovingly with a nonbeliever.

The work before a mission trip or entering the neighborhood is as important as what will occur on the field. Have a willingness to step in and lead the local church into God's vision to reach the lost locally and around the globe. Developing a solid prayer lifestyle will inoculate participants against the fowler's snare as he tries to discourage and dissuade the team from serving others in the community.

## Expand the Kingdom

For nearly a century, the North American church had its spiritual pulse on its checkbook and not on the actual needs around the globe. Many denominations have been the financial breadwinners of seeding future ministry in others' mission fields. While the model of sending funds and a limited number of people to different cultures worldwide to serve has been essential, many churches failed to invest at home in their neighborhoods. One has to ask: Can the mission field be near and far? The simple answer is yes. The church can and must tackle investing locally and worldwide to spread the gospel because God is needed everywhere. God calls the church to serve in these dark spots in your neighborhood, city, or state. Begin to look around you and find out where God has been pushed aside, ignored, or outright not wanted. That is where God is calling the church.

Expanding the kingdom is about taking back territory that the church has allowed the devil to have a field day. But not anymore; it's time to develop his kingdom, and it begins with you and your local church. There is a large portrait of Jesus knocking at the door in an office at the church, seeking to come in (Rev 3:20). While the image is in an outdated frame, the framing of Jesus knocking and seeking to enter the home (our church) resonates today. Jesus is knocking on the hearts of his church to see if they will become the church he desires for them to be in this season of ministry.

Will you or your church unlock the keys to future ministry and let him come in and provide direction?

## WHERE IS GOD LEADING

Looking back at the first two decades of this new century, it is becoming clear that the church's function is changing, but its mission stays the same. What seemed normal is abnormal, and the church is learning to shift and change directions to expand the kingdom of God. In the coming months, God will use the knowledge gleaned from the pages of this book to spark a renewal of your spirit to see where he is at work and where he is calling you to serve. By putting your certainty in Christ, he will guide the local church and thus your leadership to reach your community like never before. Some have suggested that the road before the church is facing uncertainty. Some have said the church's best days are in the past, but by now, you know our heart, we believe that the best days are out ahead, and it begins with you.

Begin to pray. Begin by setting aside this book at the end of this chapter and seek God's direction for your life and ministry. Take your time. Do not rush to jump into the next chapter. First, seek his will. Seek his direction. Write down what he tells you or what you sense in your spirit. Then ask God through your prayers, by searching the Scriptures, to allow the Holy Spirit to guide you as you seek his missional call for your life and church. See where he leads you and your local church to enter the mission field and live a life on mission. Embrace the windshield in front of you, the church's future is bright.

## MISSIONAL MOMENTS:

1. What areas are open for the local church to expand the kingdom through service activities in the community through the investment of time, talent, and treasure?

2. Where in the community is low-hanging fruit where the church can come alongside a nonprofit organization, festival, or government and serve?

3. What model does our local church use concerning missions (one-and-done, or long-term partnerships) and how can we move towards long-term partnerships? And with who?

# Chapter 5

# Telling the Missional Story
## Kingdom Impact

WE LIVE IN A day and time where people wish they could travel back in time. The mindset of going back to the "good ole days" is not new. It has been around since the beginning of time. There have always been people who have looked back to the past as they found themselves in uncomfortable positions. They failed to recognize that in the uncomfortable is where God lives. Nowhere in Scripture did God say following him would be easy. The Gospels remind the reader that Jesus had twelve close followers, one betrayed him, ten died for him, and one was placed in boiling water and put in jail for an extended period of his life. Yet far too many churches and leaders are looking for an easy way to build a church and fill its pews. If there were an easy way to live on mission, we would all be doing it already. However, the cost of following Jesus is not easy. Where did you or anyone else think serving as a missionary would be easy?

Everywhere you look today, there is a need that can only be filled through the love of Jesus. God is calling you and your local church to join the most significant missional movement of all time, share the gospel with others, and win the lost by depopulating hell. God calls you to be the living embodiment of the church and reach the lost with the gospel in new and creative ways. Think about it this way, the most incredible missional movement known to humanity is found in the Bible. Through the moving of the Holy Spirit, he is calling you to serve your community and make the words come alive.

## SEE THE NEED AROUND THE CHURCH

In the eastern part of the Appalachian Mountains sits the town of Pulaski, Virginia. For over 130 years, on the corner of fifth and Washington has sat a majestic Lutheran Church overlooking the town. For nearly three decades, Pastor Terrie Sternberg has used her longevity of service to serve the community around her. The town of Pulaski was once a bustling industrial center where passengers filled the train station for a day of shopping in the busy downtown center or families boarded the train to head back to their rural holler with packages from the day's adventures.

Over time the battery plant, warehouses, and furniture factory closed, forcing some families to move away in search of a living wage. What settled in their place was a ghost town of "what was" with a poverty rate of nearly 25 percent, strangling future hopes of "what could be." Undaunted by the negative image of abandoned buildings and poverty, the pastor at Trinity Lutheran strove to become a fixture in the community by serving on community boards, interacting with governmental leaders, and being a champion for the area. So, what led a transplant to become so ebbed into her adopted community?

### Prayer Evangelism

As the church aged with the town, they had to adapt to the given needs of its members and what they were witnessing as they traversed their town. They did not know what to do as members moved away or died off, and hardly any replaced them. They began to pray during special prayer meetings, and in their weekly services, God would show them a way to reach the needs around them. As the church was strategically overlooking the downtown and beyond, members would stand in the prayer garden or the church parking lot and pray over the community. Through intentional prayer times, God began to open the doors for the members to interact with people who did not look or act like them. While challenging at times, these God moments created opportunities for the church to witness the emerging needs that surrounded them.

## Action Steps: Pray Intentionally

Trinity Lutheran was willing to humble themselves and seek the face of God. Is God calling you or your local church into the mission field? If so, where is your prayer center? Where is the place you seek God daily? Seek to establish a prayer center where you and your church can seek God's vision for the future.

1. Be intentional: Develop intentional prayer times in large corporate gatherings, small groups of less than five, and private prayer times.

2. Be seeking: Seek God's vision for the local community and how you and the church could partner to serve his sheep.

3. Be willing: Have a generous heart to go into the places that make you uncomfortable.

4. Be a yes: When God calls, stay in an open posture to obey God's will and direction.

## Practical Evangelism

Pastor Terri led her people from a prayer posture to an outward posture. The church realized rather quickly that other agencies were not meeting some basic needs or outside organizations within their community. The church would partner with others to see needs met as they respected the family or person seeking help.

Trinity expressed a loving posture that strove to meet the person's basic needs standing in front of them through love and understanding. This practical evangelism looks away from legalism (judging the character and conduct of a person/situation) that non-Christians believe the church judges outsiders by. While messy at times, evangelism can be rewarding, and Trinity was eager to find this out.

## Action Steps: Seek Intentionally

1. Be obedient: Obey God's prompting to others in the places where others have overlooked them.

2. Be engaged: Engage with other community stakeholders to serve and support the community's critical needs.

3. Be able: Enable yourself or the church to be in a position to help others.

4. Be a promoter: Let the community and others know the church is willing and able to serve in certain volunteer spots that need to be filled by agencies in the community.

## Missional Evangelism

For over one hundred years, Trinity impacted the community in various ways. Still, in this new season of ministry, the church understood they had to be intentional about reaching those in need or who needed help in the community. If there is a desire of God's people to serve missionally, God will provide away. Trinity saw their town as an opportunity zone to serve as the hands and feet of Jesus. From putting together backpacks for a weekend food program, reading to children in local schools, to supporting beautification efforts around the community, Trinity became the face of compassion and became Jesus to a lost society.

Trinity did not develop innovative programs or projects that had to be accomplished, but they were willing to "do" something to advance the kingdom. Far too many churches choose to "talk" about serving and forget to help their neighbors.

## Action Steps: Serve Intentionally

1. Be Jesus: Be an example of Christ to others around you.

2. Be bold: Do not allow a "no" to stop you or the church from being a "yes" for others in need.

3. Be focused: The goal is not to win people to your church but to win them to Jesus.

4. Be community-based: Focus on the needs of others and allow the Holy Spirit to guide the church as you serve others in the community.

If a century-old church can reshape its missional focus and find new life in the community, could your church too? You are called to be the missionary in the harvest field of your community to meet people and share the gospel with them. You know the culture. You know the practical side of the people you will interact with, and you have already invested in the relational aspect of the people's lives by being a part of the community. This inroad in the community, through your understanding of the community, will help you and the church see the needs and then reach them more effectively than an outside pastor coming into the community as the so-called savior of the local church.

God is calling you to reach his people. God is calling you to reach the lost right where you are. God is calling you to activate your giftings in the field he's called you to live and serve in. It is not by accident that you live in your neighborhood or serve at your current church. God has divinely placed you there to be an impact maker for the kingdom. Trinity saw the gap in the community, and as a church, they moved to bridge the gap. If you do not bridge the gap in your local community, you will die and close the church.

Please recognize that you have to build relationships, and it takes time and effort. Will you be willing to spend the time to make the long-term partnerships that will lead to change?

## LIVING THE JESUS STORY OUT

The story of Trinity is not unique to the faith tradition that they belong to. The story of a transformed church has been around since the New Testament days, and it can happen to your church if you are willing to lead the effort. Think about it this way, Trinity was ready to recognize the decline in their midst and seek a way out. Is your church? Far too many churches in North America ignore the warning signs that death is near. Still, with a willing and prayerful spirit, churches facing death can grow again by living out the Jesus story in their community.

## Own Your Story

The church you serve has a beautiful story to tell. The richness found in the established church is present within the stories that cry to be unmasked and revealed for all to hear. Within her walls are stories of past lives impacted through ministry and gospel effectiveness. While those stories have seeped into the background over time because of church-related issues, you have a creative opportunity to bring them back to life by retelling past God moments. When you do this, you honor God. You also observe the memories that have been left behind by the saints who have come before.

The goal of an effective missional leader is to know the story of the past, present, and future better than anyone else in the church. Share lives changed, redemption stories, and how the church can still impact the community around them. Resetting the missional account connects to who she (the church) once was and where she is going in the future. The future for your local church is vital if you can help narrate the story of God's guidance through the decades and enable the church members to see where God has been at work all along.

## Live the Story

Too often, church members get bogged down, reminiscing about all the past mistakes and failures. Instead of getting caught in the mire of negativity, turn the attention to where God is already at work. Begin to live that life story. Every church has a positive story. Every church is doing something that is God-honoring. You might have to look harder for some, but God is there if you dig long enough. There is a powerful awakening when you realize that God is working amid the mess. There is a message of hope for the season your church is entering if you all will stay focused on what desires he has for the neighborhood around the church.

Living the story is being an example to others. When the report is negative, be the positive story maker. When voices of negativity speak about all the things not being done, be the storyteller who shares what is being accomplished in Jesus's name.

## GOD IS IN THE STORY

If you think of it, every family and every person in the family has a story that is interwound to each other. While each story has a different beginning and ending, the stories connect through DNA. The local church's story is not about who is or is not serving on the mission, but it is a story of where God is working and walking alongside each person in the church. Recently in Ashland, Kentucky, a local association closed another church. The same story plays out all over America; over time, the church's members moved away or died off, and there were not enough new members to sustain their numbers. For some, they would say, "this is the failure of faith." Others have said, "they left God, and he left them." In reality, they stopped sharing the story of God moving in their midst with their family and friends. They stopped evangelizing. They stopped seeing Jesus in the lost and broken people of the community. Could your church be next? Today the former church has been stripped of its adornments. The church has now become office space. The story of this church is a warning for all local churches. It was not one significant decision that marked this church's demarcation to closure but a series of decisions made over time that led it to close its doors.

## PLANT A SEED

For eighty years, Summit Nazarene has weathered trials and experienced fantastic triumphs. In the low times, the people sought comfort and direction in Jesus. In the high times, the people celebrated Jesus. The thread that ties eight decades in the life of Summit together is Jesus. Without Jesus, Summit would not exist.

In January 2021, the church leadership focused on Jesus as lockdowns and government mandates challenged the church's sense of direction. With fewer people and fewer resources, the administration decided to plant seeds for a future harvest. The board hired a new youth pastor within the month, and plans were approved to design and build a new youth wing in an unfinished part of the church. Instead of waiting for a decline, the board voted to seed the ground for a future growth harvest. The people joined in praying for a new crop of teen converts to the faith, a renewed presence of the Holy Spirit over the program, and a passionate commitment to living heart holiness. Since that time, twenty-five total teens have invited Jesus into their hearts, with fourteen teens making professions of faith this church year.

Even in a season of uncertainty, if a church is willing to dream, pray, and seek after God, he will provide for the needs of those who ask. Be thankful that an eighty-year-old church keeps planting seeds for a future harvest.

Hear our heart; God is in the stories left untold. Tell the stories. Share the stories with those willing to hear how God is moving. God still has more for your church to accomplish. The question is, are you ready to do the hard work to receive the reward?

## MISSIONAL MOMENTS:

1. Who have you asked God to open the door with to share the gospel? How are you praying for them daily?

2. Who are you sharing the story of God's redemption with? What are your next steps?

3. Who are you planting the seed of faith with and how are your preparing for next steps in sharing the gospel with them?

# Chapter 6

## Informing the Children
### Unilateral Effects on the Whole Church

FOR THE BOOK'S FIRST part, we focused on adults leaving their pews and engaging people outside the church's walls. But what about children? You have heard the expression that "children are our future." This overused cliché has been in existence since children were born. Life cycles abound—thus, the circle of life continues unabated from Christianity and the reality of the world around us. The future becomes a legacy, leaving the church looking like the world. Think about it this way, all generations have positive and negative issues that shape and influence their lives. Environments full of change, the unstableness of homes, or perhaps supportiveness from a child's family. Ironically, all children's futures become the legacy of caregivers, the church, and society. Depending on how their lives are shaped, they will either leave a benevolent legacy or one that may be complicated.

Children come into the world with no preconceived ideas or notions when they are born. Their worlds are shaped by watching and listening to others. Observational learning occurs by whom they are around or interact with over the early years. Behavior is learned from the environment they are born into and the space they are raised. Vygotsky's theory of "zone of proximal development" tells us that the best environment to encourage healthy cognitive development for a child is when their parents, caregivers, teachers, etc., give them a well-rounded range of tasks.

Children are products of the values their parents or guardians deem essential. Suppose the parents/guardians think that church is important. In that case, this mindset becomes a priority in their lives, or at least they understand that church is essential and becomes the foundation for the future adult to build on when they get older. Kids are resilient. The best example of seeing resilience in children is when I (Charlotte) taught military children at a Department of Defense school system. These students were so used to change. Their parents would deploy for months, sometimes as much as a year at a time. They had to cope with constant change and anxiety about their security and safety.

The pandemic changed how church is done; in many ways, it will never be the same as it was. Children deal with those changes better than adults because their knowledge base is less developed. Taking advantage of this lack of preconceived mindset is the perfect time to educate. Maybe adults in the church can learn from a child that change is not the end but can be the beginning of something new and exciting.

## CHILDREN AND MISSIONS

Why do we want children to know about missions? Key findings in a 2019 research study involving 1200 children's leaders found that two out of three Christians came to faith before the age of eighteen.[1] Stop and reflect on that number. Forty-three percent came to Christ before the age of twelve, and less than one-fourth of current believers came to Christ after the age of twenty-one. The moment of opportunity for accepting Jesus and being a Christian is far greater in younger generations than in adulthood.

1. Tony Kummer, "Children's Ministry Statistics (2019) How do Kids Come to Christ?" (Feb 17, 2022, https://ministry-to-children.com/childrens-ministry-statistics/).

A survey was given to children and youth workers that asked, "In your ministry, what is the ONE THING that is most effective in helping kids come to Christ?" Here are some responses provided.

- Talking to them about what it means to live for Christ.

- Giving them opportunities to experience God, not just learn about him.

- Teaching about Jesus's love for them.

- Showing love to kids first—accepting and letting them know they matter. That opens their hearts to hear the message of Jesus.[2]

So, it is not surprising that the number one consensus among children workers regarding understanding the importance of bringing kids to salvation *is* that childhood is when most people find Jesus.

## Children Need Jesus

Scripture records in Matt 28:18–20, "All authority in heaven and on earth that has given to me. Therefore, go and make disciples of all nations, baptizing them in the name of the Father and of the Son and the Holy Spirit, and teaching them to obey everything I have commanded you. And surely I am with you always, to the very end of the age." The fulfillment of the Great Commission is for everyone. There is no doubt about what our purpose in life is. Being a Christian means we are to model telling others about Jesus authentically. Reaching and teaching children is vital for the cause of missions because if we don't train, we are not doing as God commands.

Traditionally, children have been taught about accepting Jesus and living a Christian life in a traditional children's church or Sunday School setting. The recent pandemic, where such activities

2. Tony Kummer, "Children's Ministry Statistics (2019) How do Kids Come to Christ?" (Feb 17, 2022, https://ministry-to-children.com/childrens-ministry-statistics/).

were paused or eliminated, caused a significant loss of opportunity to train children. Today, our known methods of doing missions have significantly changed, so we have to adapt to a new "normal" that many say is uncertain.

## SHAPING THE YOUNG FOR A LASTING RELATIONSHIP WITH JESUS

There are some basic principles about children when creating a mission mindset in them that the local church should understand and adapt to.

### Children Are Trainable

The influences on their lives are what shape them. The environment they have been raised in is sometimes why they must encounter positive Christian influences as they grow and interact with the local church. The church can teach them about God, the Bible, Christian life, and ministering to others as they grow in God's grace over time.

Think about it this way, when the seed of missions is planted at an early age, the future for missions becomes brighter. Missions becomes transferable and transformable when a child who grows into an adult keeps planting new seeds in others.

### Children Can Be Empathetic

Children have to learn about empathy to administer empathy. Self-centeredness decreases when the focus is on others. Think about that as an adult. That virtue is needed in your heart too. When children begin to see needs far more significant than theirs, it broadens their scope to include others and begins to share the Jesus's compassion they have received from the local church.

The Virginia District of the Church of the Nazarene involves children who come to family camp to participate in a fundraiser for an annual district-wide compassion project. In its twelfth year, projects have focused on children with very little near and far. When Charlotte's grandson heard about the reason for the project, he was full of questions about "why" they had so little. He instantly went into the "I want to help them" mode and was on a mission to improve their lives. His value system changed when he realized his bounty compared to theirs. That could be your grandchild or the children in your church. Teach about missions and watch their hearts expand for others.

## Children Are Impressionable

If you want missions to continue, the church must expose children of all ages to what happens on the mission fields. Numerous stories have been told about missionaries who are serving *because* they *heard* a missionary tell about their missional experience. Hosting a missionary is not "old school" but vital to planting the seed in a future missionary's heart.

Children are born with an emotional sensitivity—they explore feelings of frustration, excitement, nervousness, elation, interest, and many more. But by the time they become adults, many have been hardened by society and life choices. In a study by Vandeyar (2021), children can show the epistemology of compassion and implement a pedagogy of compassion, which is why the local church and you, in particular, should be exposing global mission opportunities at least several times a year inside the church.[3] Charlotte's eight-year-old grandson recently attended a dinner/church service that featured a Cambodian missionary. The missionary showed a few pictures and shared her life and work there. Some of it was not pleasant due to that country's history, but she told about the positive, life-changing experiences that many of these people had when they became Christians—thus, the reason she is serving there. When she opened up the opportunity for questions,

3. Saloshna Vandeyar, "Pedagogy of Compassion: Negotiating the Contours of Global Citizenship" (*Journal of Research in Childhood Education* 35.2, 2021), 200–214.

her grandson was eager to ask many questions that ranged across several feelings of emotion. He wanted to know more! Rarely have we seen children not respond, in some way, to hearing about missions. Sometimes this may not be visible to you, but God sees what is stirring in their hearts.

## Children Need Exposure to Missions

Exposing children to missions in person, by electronic connection, or by reading/hearing the stories enables the Holy Spirit to stir emotions so that God can work in their hearts and, over time, might captivate the child's mind into a calling on their lives. When children hear stories about how God provides in his unique and timely ways, lives begin to be transformed. Charlotte's parents served as special assignment missionaries to Australia; they could never figure out how they lived on such a meager salary. Still, God always provided for their needs and helped them to accomplish their mission. You can't believe these things unless you hear someone (a missionary) talk about how God provides or has provided. Only God can orchestrate this. That is why children must hear from missionaries as part of a service.

Children can never run far from the call of God in their lives, but if they cannot hear the call because the local church has not allowed the call to be made, whose fault is it? The children or the local church? Not all children will be called to become missionaries in a foreign land, but ALL children can serve and live a missional lifestyle. This exposure to missions provokes or embodies the expression of emotion, whether they are affected, moved, touched, acted upon, enthusiastic, or influenced.

## Children Have to Be Taught to Give

The carnal nature of people says to gain all you can. Work hard, and keep all of it for yourself and your pleasures. But a child can be motivated and hear the call through compassion. Some may say this is manipulation. We say it is the moving and work of the Holy Spirit. Children who see adults sowing into kingdom work understand that giving is essential. Modeling is critical in developing a mission mindset and the earlier the better in transforming hearts and minds for Jesus.

Our method of teaching is different. Ask any school teacher if they have had to adapt what they teach depending on the child or school year. In the church, we, too, must adapt how we tell children about missions. Traditionally, the methods we used are no longer doable. We must find nontraditional ways to share the act of "missioning." In today's environment, since the pandemic took hold, how giving takes place (electronically or buckets in the back of the church) is hindering how our children and youth view the "giving" process. A time not too long ago, when a church received the offering, it was through an offering plate passed through the congregation. Today that can look very different.

## Visible Giving

While many churches still take a physical offering, or at least verbally, the different approach means that mission giving must adapt and change also. We like to think about it this way: giving is a demonstration of worship; thus, it involves acts of love. When children and youth see this support of a "love" offering, they associate it with a show of being missional. At Summit Church in Ashland, Kentucky, twice a year, they buy a pizza to be delivered to the church. Pizza is not the focus. The delivery driver is. When the delivery driver comes into the service, they are ushered onto the stage for the pastor to pray over them and ask do they have a need. Once the need is known, an offering bucket is placed on the steps of the stage. The pastor then asks the congregation (young and old) to give. Each time this missional investment has been made, over $500-$900 has been sowed as a tip for one pizza. What is that? That is the church being missional.

It would be advantageous for churches to practice actual giving, even if it is not standard. For the electronic givers, showing the child with you your giving on your phone might be an answer. But, they must SEE it. Charlotte shares that one day, her technologically savvy son-in-law was in church when an offering was requested for a missional need. Her grandson watched his step-father give electronically and was really "wowed" by how much he gave. Kids need to be "wowed" by sacrificial giving once in a while. God can turn a "wow" into a miracle! Let them *see* you give.

## Adapting to the New Reality

You have probably noticed that the church you grew up in or pastored in for the last few years is different. Surprised? Do not be. The church has had to adapt to changing governments, rulers, and other outside interventions for centuries. So when you view the practical side of missions, do not view it from the prism of the past but the current reality in the boarder context that the church finds herself.

The church's future is not built on yesterday but on how Scripture is carried forward today. The future you wanted yesterday is here today. The future you wish for tomorrow is now. The time for change is upon the local church. Will she adapt? Will you adapt to the changing times and claim the mantle of living your life on mission by planting seeds of faith, hope, and compassion in the church for tomorrow?

## HOW DO YOU SOW MISSIONS INTO A CHILDREN'S DEPARTMENT?

There are several simple ways to educate children about missions by tapping into modern methods of receiving and sharing information. Let us encourage you to speak with other local missionary leaders, pastors, or church officials. Seek creative ways they are reaching the children and then retrofit them to meet the needs of your children.

## Make Missions Real

Use the internet or social media as a God tool to teach, learn, and train future missionaries in your local church's care. The capacity for instant connection with people in most of the world gives children a natural way to communicate through providers such as Zoom, Skype, or WhatsApp. Arrange a time for the children to talk to a real missionary worldwide about what they do. Or you can still do it the old-fashioned with postcards, cards, and letters. But, whatever you do, do something to engage the world.

## Share the Needs

Compassionate acts stir the heart, and an emotional attachment connects to the heart to give. There are many needs in the world today, and if you look closely, even in your community. You have an excellent opportunity to raise awareness of actual conditions in and around the church. Take the missional challenge to challenge your church and children to buy a life-changing bicycle for someone in Cambodia, for example. Find a big project, and watch our big God show up. We promise the children/church will never forget giving to make life better for someone.

## Adopt a Missionary

How do you make a long-term impact? Develop a long-term relationship with a missionary and the local church. Relationship-building reinforces the connection and makes missions a real thing. In a world fraught with change, a positive side effect is that change has enabled the world to reach the church doors. Simply put, bring the culture to them.

The church can leverage the connection through electronic means (email, teleconferencing, and social media) to create an intimate connection between the missionary and the local church. When the missionary is on home assignment, they can plan on coming for an in-person visit. Year after year, deepening the relationship will strengthen the connection and idea of missions in a child's heart.

## Seize the Natural Opportunities

There will be a day when the missionary will come home—what an exciting time to connect in person with them. In the past, they visited churches telling their stories, showing pictures (slides), and raising support. Today, they do the same but in different ways. Missionaries become very real, and their duties become clear when children meet with them. Provide a time when the missionary and family can speak directly with the children. See this as another seed opportunity to plant the missionary flag in their hearts as they learn firsthand about the calling to be a missionary.

And remember, leader, no question is out of bounds. Do not be embarrassed by children's inquisitive nature and creative questions. How will they learn if they do not ask?

## Children Must Learn to Pray

You, by now, know there is power in a praying people. God can and does answer prayer. Prayer cultivates humility. Praying for missionaries is a way children can see the mission field from their worldview. They can see the purpose of why we have missionaries. Do not be afraid to have a child pray. It might seem simple to you, but it will be powerful to God. Parents should include missionaries and their needs when praying at mealtimes, before going to sleep, or before they go to school. Pray for a need and allow them to ask questions. Missionary needs should be discussed and exposed so that they know of them. Be the example, and watch the little eyes and ears follow your spiritual leadership.

Missions are only as valuable as they are shared. Please encourage them to begin their own missional story. The church will not survive if there are no children to follow. Churches must include a focus that not only seeks to bring them to a saving knowledge and action of salvation but a focus that teaches and breathes the Great Commission.

## ALL CHILDREN CAN DO MISSIONS

A blanket statement such as "all children can do missions" is very true. Youth growing up in a missions-focused church are exposed to what missions are. A child who does not grow up in that environment can learn that "helping others" is intrinsically rewarding and has a "feel good" after-effect. Even those children who don't have the best environment can understand when benevolence is kind and good to them. Children are born with a readiness to learn. The adults that surround them are the ones who impact their future. If they see that adults practice good manners, they will mimic the same. If their adult role model shows negativity to certain stimuli, like missions, the children will likely model the exact behavior of negativity.

## MISSIONAL EMPOWERMENT: EDUCATIONAL LEARNING THEORIES

You probably have heard it, and maybe you said it; we don't know what to do with children and missions. There are three factors to help you and your church understand how missional empowerment works. Let us help you develop a missional empowerment plan that will impart missional zeal in children and relieve your worry about not knowing what to do.

## Bandura's Basic Principles of Social Learning Theory

This premise is based on five steps of cognitive development with children. These are, in order, observation, attention, retention, reproduction, and motivation. In a study by Kanhadilok and Watts (2014) gives insight about some key observations emphasizing the role of adults in developing the learning process in children.

Children learn what is important by being observed (coaching, mentoring), take-up (adults modeling to the children), needing to explain (teaching process), being challenged (giving positive feedback to motivate), gaining a fresh perspective (seeing other possibilities), being encouraged to take risks (expecting results from God), and reconstruction of tacit knowledge (new knowledge being built from the whole experience).[4] The role of any adult, whether that be a parent or a Sunday school teacher, has to be intentional when creating a missions-focused trajectory. It is easy to see how this works when trying to develop a mission mindset with our children, too.

## Constructivism Learning Theory

This theory is based on the idea that children take what they're being taught and add it to their previous knowledge and experiences, creating a reality that comes from intrinsic feelings about what they have learned.

## Connectivism Learning Theory

When connections are made, it increases participation and increases positive motivation for actions surrounding this new learning.

We can hear you now: "How can I apply this research and have it done practically?" Glad you asked. Here is an example: children see adults give an offering. The children understand they must sacrifice something they have for someone they do not know. This opens the conversation window to speak about why. Move them from the "why," and you can talk about the "what" of serving others. As the why and what is understood, you move to the

---

4. P. Kanhadilok and M. Watts, "Adult Play-Learning: Observing Informal Family Education at a Science Museum" (*Studies in the Education of Adults* 46.1, 2014) 23-41.

"blessing" of helping others. So the simple missional formula is why + what = blessing.

Missions can be simple, and it all starts with communication. Young or old, tell the story of Jesus calling others because you never know if he might call one from your local church.

## MISSIONAL MOMENTS:

1. What can I do? Take one small idea and build on it.

2. Share a mission's story—new AND old stories inspire and motivate.

3. Create an opportunity for kids to give toward a "missional" project.

4. Do a Zoom session with a missionary—there are many who will participate and share their story. Awareness is key in understanding what missions is all about.

# Chapter 7

## Exposing Missions to Youth/Young Adults Promotes a Changed Mindset

THE YOUTH OF TODAY are a product of many things. Their worlds are complicated. Socially, they may find it difficult to fit in. They have grown up in a highly digital environment which contributes to and hinders their ability to communicate and function with others. Social issues such as drug/alcohol use, school violence, materialism, obesity, and shifting economies intrude on their lives and they succumb by retreating and backing off which leads to a disconnection between them and the local church.

This is why it is even more important to get them to focus elsewhere on the godly things that matter in life. Young people need the investment of the local church to include them in missions locally and around the world. Missions will help them to turn their focus outward instead of on themselves and see the spiritual and relational connections around them. Where culture says, "give to me," the church should be about "give to others." Their sense of worthiness is directly related to the activities they are involved in. Think about it this way, it is difficult to feel sorry for yourself when you are pouring yourself into helping others.

Teenagers, and even young adults are on the cusp of making life decisions and the church has an important part to play over their lives. As they grow, they are sorting, evaluating, planning, experimenting, and experiencing a plethora of other influential factors that shape the rest of their lives. It is a peculiar but impressionable age that missions can become their foundation of their active faith. Through all the peer pressure and influences that abound, missions can provide them authenticity! The *real deal* is transparent but sometimes difficult to find if the church first does not invest in the next generation of leaders. Through relational and direct experiences, this generation of leaders will either leave the church or turn towards her with a passion to help others. The choice is yours. Will you help build up the missional future of your church?

## YOUTH ON MISSION

As part of this resource, a youth pastor was interviewed from a large church in Nashville, Tennessee, who recently took thirty-one ninth through twelfth grade students and chaperones on a mission's trip to Alaska. With the onset of the pandemic that struck the world the trip was put in limbo, but with creativity and divine direction the trip eventually was planned around cancellations due to the pandemic. The missional youth pastor shared that the church plans a four-year cycle of mission-type trips for the teenagers. An example of a local (national) trip was to conduct a vacation Bible school in the inner city of Cleveland, Ohio, with an international trip every fourth year. The other three years have different focuses planned on a rotating cycle, such as denominational events with national service projects. A teen who enters the youth group as a freshman can participate in each of the planned events within a four-year period. Thus, laying a strong foundation for local, national, and international missions.

During their recent trip to Alaska, the missional youth pastor asked the student to focus on one objective: *be available and be flexible.* This way expectations were not set before hand in the teens mind, and the students remained open-minded about what they were to experience. As they traversed the Alaskan frontier, some of the activities and acts of service they were involved in were volunteering to repair and paint a pastor's home, serving meals in a homeless shelter, visiting and talking in-depth with seniors who came daily to a senior community center (which, consequently, caused students to develop post-trip relationships with some of the seniors), improving a home for someone, and simply giving out bottles with scripture to anyone they encountered. Missions was not talked about or even read; it was put into practice. Do not miss this important point, the missional engagement factor is something not to gloss over. The Z and future generations wants to experience missions, rather than just give financially to missions. In the past a missionary would speak to a local church and then the pastor would ask for a special offering. Today, the offering is bodies doing the work rather than funds. For the local church to be relevant in the future, she must grasp this point, and adapt to meet the current needs of the generation she is engaging. For them (the Z and future generations), they want a church that *goes* and *does* not *stays* and *gives* by impacting the community they are a part of daily.

## STRATEGIES FOR SERVING ON MISSION

In reflecting on the most recent trip, the missional youth pastor shared the impact that the trip had on students. The word poverty was spoken of, experienced, and viewed with a new lens by the group. While they have seen inner city, and rural poverty, it surprised them to see poverty in a new light in such majestic surroundings. By getting the students outside of their comfort zone and embracing the communities they visited through the eyes of Jesus, they saw the need and examined each person with the compassion of Christ. Instead of feeling sorry for the people they encountered they experienced love and understanding through a listening ear. What was a summer trip for most, turned into a life altering missional trip.

The church in many ways is a safe haven against the outside world and this trip brought the teens face-to-face with the realities of life for many outside their own spiritual and physical bubbles. The teens saw what hopelessness and brokenness truly looked like, not from reading a book but in experiencing the reality of another person's life. The word *missions* is not stagnant, but active. Missions is about people, not just places. When you help a young person experience mission, they begin to live the mission. When they began to talk to the people, they began to experience compassion for those who had less than they did. The act of listening to the stories caused the students to begin building a relationship with people. This act of talking led to taking an interest in finding solutions that would better their lives but change their own at the same time. As the students departed their time on the last frontier, they realized that there were key strategies that they used in their missional endeavor.

## When You Meet Someone, Begin a Natural Conversation with Them

It seems natural to talk with someone you meet for the first time. But, in a highly tech savvy world, many young people do not have the skill sets or comfort level to speak with someone outside of texting or posting a picture on social media. But, teens do not need a large vocabulary, what they need is a heart for listening to cues that others will give them. They can engage by asking simple questions ("How long have you lived in this area?" or "What would you say is your favorite place to visit locally?"). Let the conversation evolve naturally and keep all information general but with an ear toward learning about the person and the culture of the community. We must caution that students should be careful not to convey too much personal information as it is not about them, but about the person that they are engaging with. Over time, encourage them to move the general relationship into a spiritual one by having the students ask before they leave the conversation, "Can I pray for you?" Some may not want prayer, and you should train your students to expect that at times, but it does raise awareness for the student and the person being asked of God, prayer, hope, and other good things of God.

## Go in Groups

You have most likely heard "there is strength in numbers." The reality is that not everyone has the gift of talking to strangers, but others who do not can certainly support those who do. Confidence is built over time by engaging. When others in a small group see the ease of speaking with a total stranger, they will begin to mirror that missional behavior, and this reality is not new for our time. Throughout the New Testament, Jesus, then the disciples, are seen instructing and serving, in pairs or more. Why? Because there is strength in numbers. Not only from a safety aspect, but a spiritual one. God has given each person the right gifting. You have the right gifting for what he has called you to do. For one it may be being a prayer warrior. For another the gift of easy conversation with strangers. Still for others, the ability to work with their hands. But, through it all, God has called his people to serve together and not live a life of spiritual isolation.

Serving collaboratively helps with spiritual confidence to be bold in witnessing with a stranger, to sharing Jesus stories of how he has changed your life, all while engaging missionally with a person you are impacting as much as they are impacting you.

## Don't Stop Serving Because the Trip Is Over

We have all been there, one-and-done service projects. But is that all that Christ has called us to do? A love for missions and thus a missional lifestyle is developed overtime, through the creation of continually missional engagement locally, or around the world. Service can spill out into many other directions, but the key word is to *serve*. As the students returned home, some were bitten by the missional bug. Now they saw their own community with fresh missional eyes. Which led some of the students to begin volunteering for their church's Emmaus group which operates within their local church. Others wanted to join volunteer clubs at the high school, while still others wanted to capture the moment and beginning planning the next step on their own missional journey.

The plan of this local church youth group is to immerse students once a year in a large missional activity. But it could easily be a monthly activity by engaging a local senior center, soup kitchen, pregnancy center, or service organization such as Kiwanis, Lions, or Rotary Clubs. Whatever you do, keep in mind that missions is action, so get doing, rather than thinking about where to help next.

## Develop a Service Mindset

Service is engaging in helping someone in need. Small or large, there are service projects in and around your church's neighborhood. From repainting park benches, fixing a handicap ramp at a home, or serving hot chocolate during the Christmas parade, service opportunities abound. The spirit of service should not be just once a year, but a lifestyle of giving back what God has given to you. A simple way to facilitate service opportunities is to gather the teens around on a youth night and over pizza have them share ideas where the church can get engaged. Write them down. Pray over them. And then pick a few out that can be done as a group. The seed planted on the last missional trip or activity will never leave their minds if you help keep missions front and center.

After each service project, find ways to share the story of how the act of service impacted each teen or the group as whole. This can be done on Sunday morning testimony time, a creative video to be shared in service and on social media, or even stories written to the local newspaper or online with a picture of the activity. These acts reinforce what has taken place and begins to cement in the minds of the youth, that their service activity mattered.

## Always Pray for Those You Connect With

Prayer must be the foundational anchor of each service project. Pray before. Pray during. Pray after. We call this strategy *P3*. Throughout Jesus's life he sought times of public and private prayers. He prayed alone, in small groups, and large groups. He prayed for needs, and desires. He prayed with compassion, and care. The anchor of his ministry was prayer. If it's good for Jesus, it should be good for us. Regardless of confidence level prayers can be done. For some, praying naturally can be out loud, but for others, privately. But, whatever you do, pray! Prayer crystallizes the reason the trip or missional activity was done in the first place. Prayer quiets the soul, renews the spirit, challenges the findings, and explores the new horizons.

In missional engagements as you pray with someone that you have been interacting with you are creating an opening for the Spirit of God to impact two lives (yours and the one you have prayed for). God will use these openings to move in each of your lives and make the relationship stronger.

## SQUARING THE ROOT OF MISSIONS

If you can direct a young person into missional acts of service, they can begin to see how it affects the whole world. They will begin to see how significant they are in benefiting others. This concept moves them from an inward focus to an outward posture and gets them connected in the spiritual community of the church. The question we are most often asked from those who want a youth group to be missional focused is "how?" It is a simple question, yet not always practical when reflected on. Let us try to break it down into four squares of our imaginary missional pie.

## Square One: Involve Them in a Mission Trip

"But how?" you might be saying to yourself. When you engage with your church's youth outside of the traditional Sunday norms, you will begin to develop a deeper relationship with them beyond the surface level norms of Sunday morning or Wednesday night. These outside missional engagements can be local or global. Our encouragement is to trust your spiritual instincts. Find a need in the community and connect with that need by going and doing. Find a need in the world and connect through social media, Zoom, or some other creative technology. Locally it can mean helping your neighbor or it can be connecting long term through a church-community partnership. Globally it could be adopting a church or project in another part of the world. Whatever you do, do something!

We want to commend youth leaders that make it a priority to always incorporate a missions-type activity for their youth groups. Small or large, when missions is introduced and shared time and time again, that seed of faith begins to grow in the hearts of the teens. It becomes a springboard for developing a servant's spirit. It instills the value of missions in the life of an early believer and primes the spiritual pump for what is to come in their walk with Christ. As the youth come back from each outside missional gathering, debrief with them. Ask questions, such as what worked well? Where did you feel like you had a breakthrough? Where did you feel you hit a spiritual wall? What did you enjoy the most? What could have been done better? Is God calling you to help more or not?

These questions and those you come up with will provide opportunities for you to hear feedback and create a space where youth groups feels their opinion is valued in the broader conversation relating to missions.

## Square Two: Present the Opportunity

An opportunity not presented is an opportunity lost in not sharing missions. Nudge if you have too. Charlotte remembers an unprecedented opportunity given at a church camp one year that exemplifies impromptu action. The youth leader talked about how some people in other countries didn't have clean water available to them in an underprivileged country. One interested youth began asking questions which led to more questions. Events led to these youth deciding this was an important thing to do and they gave out of love to make a difference in this situation. The amount raised was phenomenal and all because the opportunity was presented.

A simple idea shared might be the next God idea that transforms the lives of thousands. Be obedient when the Holy Spirit prompts. Allow opportunities to be prayed over, shared, disseminated for feedback, and then put into action. God has a master plan that you might only see a portion of for your youth group. Trust the God process that comes through prayer: seek, listen, discern, and obey. Four steps that come out presenting a God idea.

## Square Three: Engage Them in Conversation about Life Contributions and Service

This is such an important time to listen and encourage. When the focus becomes *outward* instead of *inward* their whole perspective changes. Conversations open the soul to receive the heart of God for them and thus the local church. Lives will be transformed when the transformer (God) is allowed in. Be encouraged today missional leader, God is not done with you, your local church, or the teens that are rising to claim the mantle of missional engagement. By encouraging the youth group to expand their horizons they will begin to capture the God dream that is being placed inside of them. Think about it this way, through missional engagement a future missionary, or a missionary president, may be in your midst. How exiting to think of the prospect!

As you see one who is called or a group tells you they are called into missional service, begin to mentor them. Maybe not you alone but find someone in your church who you trust. Develop a team of older adults who are willing to be investors of this future missional seed. Through meaningful engagement, lives will be changed for the better.

## Square Four: Nurture

The word "nurture" can be used as a verb or a noun. The action of the word indicates that care and encouragement is engaged. The noun indicates the process of doing. Growing, succeeding, and developing are all needed to help someone on a missional journey. The verb implies that an emotion of caring is involved. It is hard to serve without the act of being compassionate. Nurturing the call to missions cannot start early enough. Early adolescence is a time of great developmental change and challenge. Many say that this is a critical period of their lives where the influences of the world begin to shape their future. It is during this period that youth need to cultivate empathic trajectories. Their social cognition abilities are being developed through this time and it is the time that they need to exercise empathetic behavior. If they can begin to understand and feel empathy as children, then this is an easier task to build on, but our youth need to experience acts that exemplify a "pay it forward" mentality or feel a connectedness to something. Good parenting helps them to see this but so many teens/youths lack good parenting models and need positive and Christian advocates, and if that is not the case, the church has great opportunity to provide that nurturing community.

This is why missionally focused church youth groups are needed. Never underestimate how extremely important Christian youth ministry is! The mission-focused procedures and activities experienced within a body of young Christians will never leave their mindset and will help them as well as help your local church to stay missional.

## MISSIONAL MOMENTS:

1. What can I do? Do SOMETHING! What is it that you can do to share missions?

2. While it is best to train children to be missional never assume that it is unimportant to engage youth in missional activity.

Where can you engage children with missions inside your local church?

3. The impact of involving youth can be life-altering for them. *Simple acts* of sharing Jesus to others takes the focus off of themselves and looks to others. How can you share Jesus with others through simple acts?

# Chapter 8

# Generational Missions
## Recapturing Service across All Age Groups

IT IS NOT UNCOMMON to hear about "generational missions" today. Let us define the term "generational missions" if you have yet to understand the jargon. *Missions that are active across all age groups and demographics that places serving together over generational silos.* For far too long in the North American church, we have focused too much on *how* missions gets done and not enough effort on *who* is doing missions. God is not calling one group to serve; he is calling ALL. If the church is going to *be the church*, all members must play their part in helping the larger vision of winning lost souls.

When was the last time your local church did a missions project with all age groups helping? If you have, celebrate because your church is part of a select few serving like Jesus. If we are honest with ourselves, many churches are struggling with developing a missions program that keeps everyone awake, much less focusing on reaching all generations. Instead of seeing a lack of foundational missional movement in the church, see it as an opportunity to revamp the way missions are preached, presented, and finding creative ways to partner with others.

## PREACH WITH PASSION AND TELL THE STORY

What makes people excited about missions? A mission president or pastor who is enthusiastic about missions. Pretty simple. A boring leader will have dull results. As the pastor or local mission president, if you are not excited about missions, then the people in the pews will also not be excited about it. The local church needs missional leaders that will exude a love for missions. There is something relational that happens in the local church's life when two or more are gathered; God shows up and transforms the old and creates a new spirit. When you share the gospel in a way that connects with someone's hands and feet, you are enabling and challenging them to become Jesus in the community.

As a leader in the church, you have an incredible opportunity to share what you are passionate about in the church. If you are passionate about missions, your people will become passionate about missions, from interweaving missional anecdotes into sermons or on the worship card to developing missional outreach projects where church members can be the church in action. This will develop a cumulative effect over time that will help the church reengage in missions locally.

## Present the Missional Journey as a Long-Term Engagement

The idea of one-and-done missional services or projects must be put to rest once and for all as the church begins to see missions as the thread that holds and propels the church forward. It has been said that if you take missions out of the Bible, all you have left will be the covers. Let's say that again for the people in the back row. Missions are integral to whom the church was created to be from its inception. Present missions as a journey of sharing, caring, learning, and adapting. Share the gospel of Christ with others you encounter daily in your normal activities. Care about everyone you meet, not just known believers. Find the unknown believers and love them like Jesus. Spend time slowing down in your busy schedule and learn from everyone you cross paths with, as they have something to teach you and vice-versa. Then as you engage with a person over time, begin to adapt their story to share God's story of how he has transformed your life. As you follow the stages of living on mission, adapt to the concept that you are to live on a mission daily, not just on national and foreign trips. Realize that your neighborhood, workplace, and schoolhouse are your mission fields.

## Partner Inside and Outside the Local Church

Ask yourself: Where is God at work already in my community? It is there where you and the church should place yourselves. For far too long, the church has thought it should start and control every aspect of programs to help the community. The reality is that the community does not want the church to manage them but to partner with them in building a healthier community. Within your local community, dozens of nonprofits need volunteers, board members, and donors. Find projects that resonate with your people and develop a long-term partnership.

As you identify community partners, incorporate cross-generational groups that bring all age groups together to work for a common good. As you do, these generational groups will learn from each other, begin to trust each other, and share life on mission. These groups will strengthen and then enhance the inside and outside local partnerships around the church.

This is an exciting time for the church to reconnect with the community outside its doors. It starts not with one age group but multiple age groups working together to share the gospel of Christ with the community.

## CONNECTING THE MISSION OF THE CHURCH WITH THE COMMUNITY

While churches focus on ministry for all generations, they should also focus on how each generation responds to and lives out the

Great Commission. Promoting a biblical worldview should include how all age groups should serve as a light to a dark world. Ideally, a local church should make its missions program an intergenerational ministry whose focus is being missional to and in the community and the world. Missions are quintessential to the foundational development of the local church and, in turn, become pleasing to God when everyone in the local church is working to help build the kingdom near and far. Realize that God blesses those who love and serve him. Psalm 145:9 reminds the reader, "The LORD is good to all: and His tender mercies are over all His works." The local church must strive to be holy and obedient. Holiness is so unique and powerful that it cannot be left to just the holiness faiths but it should be lived out regardless of denomination. Holiness should radiate from you like energy from God. Think about it this way, God will empower and bless you if you obey his commands. We do not know about you, but we want to live out that type of power in our ministry assignments, and you should too.

The missional leader understands it takes all (children, youth, and adults) to develop a mission mindset. Transformation does not happen overnight but will occur once everyone across all demographics strives to live out their daily missional tasks. Every age contributes something to the success of missions. It would help if you modeled this mission mindset for those with whom you are connected—adults, youth, and children. The whole concept of missions is SERVICE! Anyone can serve.

## Missions Is for All

Missions is worship. Giving is worship. Praying is worship. Serving is worship. Being a missionary is worship. Education is worship. Christian mission is an organized effort to spread Christianity to new converts. It is not new, but it does take action to act out the biblical calling that Christ gave his church thousands of years ago. Whatever you do through the church's mission, it should be to glorify and worship God. When the local church sees Christ in all and not some part of their activity, they will begin to live a life on mission that begins to impact the community around them.

It takes many acts to win others to Christ in our diverse and culturally different world. Remember to keep serving, even if you do not see the fruit of the labor. You must pray, give, educate, and collaborate with others to see a life or situation turn around. Transformation comes when you are obedient, not in the amount of time you put in. Trust that God is leading and working through community service; God will fill your missional account to overflowing.

Remember, ALL must participate in living on missions inside the local church. It cannot be left to the pastor or missions president. It sounds easier said than done, right? But it can be done when you trust God and do your part.

## Missions Is Service

The whole concept of missions is service. Serving others must be taught. Helping others must be done. Aiding others must be lived out as part of your everyday life. Serving people who do not look, act, or think like you is not a one-and-done activity but a long-term partnership of helping the community around you one person at a time. God's plan is for you and the local church to know him, which is his plan for the design of the church's life. God did not create the local church and people like you to sit and wait for him to return. No, he has called you, his bride, the church, to engage the community around them. Getting outside the church's walls is foundational to building lasting partnerships that transform the community and your local church for the better.

If the pandemic has taught the church anything, people matter more than programs. With the people, programs can run. Without the people, service to others cannot happen. Be challenged today to find a place in the community and serve. Please do not wait on your congregation to do it first, be the leader and share your example.

## Missions Is Being Culturally Aware

Everyone needs Jesus, but sharing the path to Jesus's grace may look different from a different perspective. Showing and conveying God's love is foundational to winning all people to Christ. As you venture from the pulpit or pew and into a community partnership, know that your role should be listening more than sharing at the beginning. As you learn about the people you are working alongside and build trust with your co-laborers, you will be able to share the gospel. See it this way, let the gospel speak through your actions and deeds, not just your words. Let the love of Christ be seen in you by showing up on time, serving with a spirit of generosity, and celebrating what others do around you. In essence, be a champion for Christ in the community.

Understand as you serve in the community, you are entering a post-Christian society, and as such, you must be culturally sensitive in how you share the gospel. Like a missionary entering a foreign field, you will join an area with challenges concerning the gospel message. At the same time, you will be familiar as a member of the broader community. As you enter uncharted territory, navigate the cultural issues in sharing the gospel today with gods grace. As with the disciples from biblical times, you will find ways to adapt, enable conversations, and pray through as God leads in the process. God is still calling his people to reach the lost with the gospel. You are doing so in a way that respects the culture—enabling Christ to be encountered through you and your local ministry.

## Missions Is NOT a "One-Size-Fits-All" Experience

There is no cookie-cutter approach to missions. We wish there were. But culturally, communally, and relationally each area differs from day to night. It is crucial to know ministry looks different for everyone. Context matters as much as the heart behind the reason for serving. If you know the context (mission field) you are entering, you give yourself a head start in serving others. If you try to come in with a one-size-fits model, you will destroy the goodwill and harm your witness for Christ.

So, while there might not be a one-size-fits all model, one model stays the same: the message of God's love. Serving on a mission is motivated by a calling, not a directive. God has called the church to live out Christlikeness in all the church members do. Each time you invest an hour of your time into someone else's life or a nonprofit agency, you invest in kingdom building that will pry spiritual dividends over time.

## SERVE—TRUST—INFLUENCE—CARE—GIVE

### How to Serve

It is hard to separate the word *missions* from the word *service*. In fact, it is hard to view Christianity that is not in alignment with serving. We are commissioned in the Scriptures that we are to witness and win the world for God. It is in our commissioning that we serve. If you are a Christian then you should be serving! *Generously* serving in some way. This may be in the form of giving money, giving time, mentoring, intentional praying, providing care, being a missionary abroad, or feeding the poor. There are unnumbered ways to serve! God prompts us to serve and the blessings received when we act upon his prompting match nothing else we can do.

### Trust

Belief in God means we can trust him with everything. We can rely on him to honor our mission efforts. Acting on a missional mindset that encapsulates service is not bad. In fact, God will use what you are doing in ways that are unimaginable. Trust God with your service. Trusting is an emotion that is incredibly powerful and will give you confidence to continue to serve.

## Influence

In your service you will be an influencer! Children who do acts of kindness are probably the easiest ones to recognize the power of influence. Their hearts are soft and tender and they don't have formed biases. When they see how they can influence and make differences in other's lives, it impacts their view. Many times they want to do more! Youth are much the same way. Their biases are stronger but they still see and feel the power of their impact. Adults can be strong influencers as well.

## Care

So many times, we do things out of obligation or routine which are not bad, but if our acts would exemplify a depth of caring then the receiver looks at you in a different light. Some words that describe this level of caring are being attentive, compassionate, concerned, benignant, and sensitive. Sometimes this begs the question, "Do I really want to make a difference in this person's life?" It takes a deeper level of commitment but maybe that is what God is wanting you to do.

## Give

Giving encompasses so many different acts. The *giving* of money, time, talents, and possessions all require a mindset of releasing something but in a way that rewards us in the giving act. Jim Elliot, infamous martyred missionary, said, "He is no fool who gives what he cannot keep to gain what he cannot lose."[1] We should daily live with the mindset of what we can give today.

C. S. Lewis once said, "There are better things ahead than any we leave behind."[2] What we do, every day for God, is about missions. Our daily walk with God should include a missions focus.

1. Jim Elliot, *The Journals of Jim Elliot* (Grand Rapids: Baker, 2002), 174.

2. C. S. Lewis, *The Collected Letters of C. S. Lewis* (San Francisco: Harper-One, 2004), 1430.

It is always a joy to listen to elderly folk who talk about the goodness of God. Wouldn't it be a wonderful thing if all people could live basking in the acts of service they have done throughout their lives? We need to cultivate a spirit of being missional as early as we can within all generations of humankind.

## RETHINK MISSIONS

Our traditional ways of doing church in the church have been upset—we have to RETHINK how to prioritize missions. Conventional methods of doing things may never exist again, but it is not the end of the missional objective. The church must learn how to find *other* and possibly better ways to minister and support the church's mission. It is essential to know that the church's mission is to share the gospel, not just to meet on Sundays. God is calling for MORE from his church, not just the status quo. The pandemic has shaken the church to its core. Through the repercussions that come from it, the church can grow closer to Christ and his mission as never before.

An exciting concept that used to exist was that *missions* were abroad—on foreign soil. But the profound truth is that missions is everywhere. It dwells in the inner city and in refugee camps that are on American soil. It is our "next-door" neighbor or the teachers teaching our children. The opportunity to do ministry avails itself all around us. The world has become smaller with the tools of technology. Instead of fearing technology, the church should embrace God's new tools to share the gospel in new and creative ways.

Today, these same types of stories are in our midst. There are older adults who want to go and serve in nontraditional ways. There are youth who have spent time in mission service before narrowing down career paths. I (Charlotte) have a friend in his early twenties who is serving in Ukraine now. His goal is to make a difference for the crisis taking place in that country. He wrote in his 9/6/2022 blog, "The past few months I have come to fall in love with a wonderful body of believers in Ukraine, and I do not say it lightly. They truly have caught my heart. It brings me great joy to announce to you that Lord willing, I will be moving to Ukraine with a one-way ticket in just one or two short months. HOW EXCITING!"[3] Use these stories and accounts to motivate others.

## MISSIONAL MOMENTS:

1. Where is God in the story of your relationship with others you are serving alongside of in the community?

2. How are you sharing the stories of others with others as a way to motivate and encourage them to join you on the missional community journey?

3. Who are you partnering with cross-generationally in helping share the story outside the four walls of the church?

3. Gabriel Montanez, "Eastward Again" (Sep 6, 2022, https://gabrielmontanez.theworldrace.org/post/eastward-again/).

# Epilogue

## Putting Missions into Practice
### Living Out the Mission

IT IS TIME TO take the thoughts and words from this resource and put them into action. There might be a temptation to read, discuss, and not doing anything with what you have just read and begun to formulate in your heart. Let us encourage you to not stop at the last period of this book but to put into action the practices found in these pages. One cannot help but to think what God can do through you, through your ministry and local church if you begin to live on mission.

### A CUP OF JOE FOR JESUS

We wrote about Summit Church earlier in this book, but we want to draw your attention to how they are doing a form of missions inside their local church. A decade ago, the church took a big step by leaving its sixty-plus-year worship space to build a new building on the same grounds. But, with that one act of faith, they rejuvenated their church to become more missional. Through the design of the building, music, preaching, and overall worship, they designed a space to reach future generations with the gospel. Over the last four years, the church has continued to transform as they have learned to be nimble due to the constraints of the pandemic and economic inflation that has affected giving and spiritual morale in the church. They have used a cup of joe with Jesus to transform conversations and, thus, lives.

## See the Need and Learn to Adapt

When the church moved into its new space in the summer of 2014, it started offering coffee and donuts in the lobby. After five years, the leadership realized that to be more welcoming, they needed to prepare for younger families, and one small way they could do that was to offer a broader selection of morning breakfast items. The breakfast area became a family favorite by adding fresh fruit, granola bars, breakfast cookies, and various juices, along with a new selection of donuts. The goal was to help young families rushing to church with one less thing to worry about on a Sunday morning. By tweaking the breakfast offerings and creating an attractive selection of items for families, the church was privately saying, "We see you, young parents. We see you, children and teens."

You might say, how is that missional? Missional engagement is intentional preparation and serving of community needs. In this case, the community is the local church. The "need" is to help facilitate providing a meal for a family in need. This simple act of caring opens the door for the parents to hear the message of heart holiness. It enables the children to learn about Jesus and missionaries alike. For the broader church, to see Jesus moving in the lives of all age groups. And for God to be glorified in the simplest acts of faith.

It is a timeless reminder that small acts turn into significant transformation actions with Jesus.

## Support Other People's Ideas

Through the interactions with current members and guests each Sunday, the coffee area helpers realized that the families wanted more coffee (hot and cold), tea flavors (hot and cold), and more breakfast choices. As more younger families invited others their age to the church, the leadership saw the need to expand their breakfast area again. In consultation with the pastor, four ladies decided to design a new "coffee house" experience in an unused classroom. They created a coffee house vibe that is fresh and attractive to newcomers and old alike through decorations of lights, high-top tables, flat-screen television that plays modern worship music, a couch, and an end table. Through specialty drinks and flavored syrup, they have used their barista skills to recreate a coffee chain vibe that has enhanced the original coffee area. Recently they added more specialty drinks (hot and cold) with creative names that church members came up with and are posted on the wall for guests to select.

Volunteers run the coffee house, have designed the feel, and purchased needed items. In recent weeks they have begun training others to help step in and serve. As a leader, the pastor saw the missional heart to connect with new and old families and cheered on this local missional endeavor. Sometimes the best thing to do as a leader is to get out of the way and allow God to move.

## Sustain the Vision by Meeting Current Realities

The reality is that the world outside the church's doors is rapidly changing. Like it or not, change has come to the church's doors. For decades the church was able to keep the world out. But as the world has changed, that change has seeped into the church. It is forcing the church to adapt or die. The local congregation can fight or adapt to meet it in a godly way. This local church (Summit) decided to adapt and change. As the church entered its eightieth year as of this writing, research says that a church that old should be on the decline. They are not. Why? Summit was willing to adapt to the times and to be more missional. Not just on the outside in serving the community, but on the inside where there sometimes is pushback to new missional ideas.

One lesson an outside observer can learn is to sustain a long-term healthy vision of the church and keep progressing forward; the church leadership has to seek God's will constantly. The change will not be easy; it is necessary to meet the needs of the current community that is around the church. Maybe your local church does not want a coffee house, but what does it want? What do you want to see happen inside and outside your local church?

Inaction is action. It stops progress and slows God's momentum in the church. There is a tendency for churches to talk things to death. Let us encourage you to pray. Seek God's will for your local church as you discover where he is at work in the community, and prepare to meet him there. Know this truth: God is not done with your local church. He will use your heart and that of others to be missionaries near and far. Regardless of age and where the church is today, God can still use a mighty remnant to transform the world.

# About the Authors

**Dr. Desmond Barrett** is the lead pastor at Summit Church of the Nazarene in Ashland, Kentucky, where he is married to his wife, Julie, and has four children. He is a former district mission president for the Kentucky District Church of the Nazarene. He is the author of *Revitalizing the Declining Church: From Deaths Door to Community Growth* (2021), *Addition through Subtraction: Revitalizing the Established Church* (2022), and coauthor of *Revitalize to Plant: Reshaping the Established Church to Plant Churches* (2023).

He is a podcasts host of the *Revitalizing the Declining Church with Dr. Desmond Barrett*, has done extensive research in the area of church revitalization, and serves as church revitalizer, consultant, coach, and mentor to revitalizing pastors and churches.

He is a graduate of Nazarene Bible College (Bachelor of Ministry), and Trevecca Nazarene University (Master of Organizational Leadership, and Doctor of Education in Leadership and Professional Practice).

**Dr. Charlotte Holter** is an adjunct professor in the School of Education at Liberty University where she teaches graduate students in Lynchburg, Virginia, district mission president for the Virginia District Church of the Nazarene, and a retired veteran elementary school teacher of thirty years. She is the coauthor of *Linking Literature to Structures: Grades 3–5* (2015) and *Linking Literature to Structures: Grades K–2* (2015).

She is a graduate of Mid-America Nazarene University (Bachelor of Arts in Elementary Education), University of West Florida

(Master of Elementary Education, Gifted Education), and Virginia Polytechnic Institute and State University (Doctor of Education in Integrative STEM Education).